YOUR NEW SAILBOAT:
CHOOSING IT, USING IT

The Editors of Chapman Piloting

Hearst Books
A Division of Sterling Publishing Co., Inc.
New York

Every effort has been made to ensure that all the information in this book
is accurate. However, due to differing conditions, tools, and individual skills,
the publisher cannot be responsible for any injuries, losses, and other damages
that may result from the use of the information in this book.

Produced by Bill SMITH STUDIO
Publisher: Jacqueline A. Ball
Art & Design: Jay Jaffe, Brad Holroyd
Production Director: Maureen O'Connor

Library of Congress Cataloging-in-Publication Data
Your new sailboat / edited by Diana B. Jessie ; Roger Marshall, contributor.
p.cm.—(A Chapman nautical guide)
ISBN 1-58816-113-7
Motorboats. I. Jessie, Diana. II. Marshall, Roger. III. Series.

VM351.Y67 2002
623.8'223—dc21   2001039864

10 9 8 7 6 5 3 2 1

Published by Hearst Books, a division of
Sterling Publishing Company, Inc.
387 Park Avenue South, New York, N.Y. 10016

CHAPMAN and CHAPMAN PILOTING and Hearst Books are trademarks
owned by Hearst Communications, Inc.

Distributed in Canada by Sterling Publishing
c/o Canadian Manda Group, One Atlantic Avenue, Suite 105
Toronto, Ontario, Canada M6K 3E7
Distributed in Australia by Capricorn Link (Australia) Pty. Ltd.
P.O. Box 704, Windsor, NSW 2756 Australia

Printed in the United States of America

ISBN 1-58816-113-7

Photo Credits: This product/publication includes images from the Corel Stock Photo
Library and PhotoDisc Digital Stock Photography, which are protected by the copyright
laws of the U.S., Canada, and elsewhere. Used under license.

Cover: G. & M. David de Lossy/The Image Bank. Pg. 33: Courtesy Lirakis Safety
Harness; pg. 66: John Whiting; pg. 78: Ed Homonylo; pg. 110: Ed Homonylo;
pgs. 112-113: Courtesy Rule Industries (Danforth); Courtesy Simpson Lawrence USA
(plow); Ed Homonylo (Bruce); Courtesy Creative Marine (Max); pg. 115: Courtesy
Simpson Lawrence USA; pg. 119: Courtesy Lewmar Marine; pg. 122: Courtesy of C&C
International Yachts; pg. 124 Courtesy Bayliner Yachts; pg. 132: Robert Chartier;
pg. 144: Robert Chartier; pg. 148: Ed Homonylo; pg. 151: Courtesy Zodiac Hurricane
Technologies; pg. 168: Philip C. Jackson; pg. 174: Ed Homonylo.

Introduction and Acknowledgments

Whether this is your first boat, or your second—or even your third or fourth—*Your New Sailboat: Choosing It, Using It* will guide you through the process of selecting and purchasing the sailboat that's exactly right for you. Whether "new" means really new or used—for there are great bargains to be had in used boats—*Your New Sailboat* offers comprehensive guidelines on what to look for in a sailboat and how to use it for maximum enjoyment and sailing pleasure.

This is the only reference guide that can take buyers in all budget ranges and of all backgrounds and experience through the process of finding their own dreamboats. You'll have the chance to assess your desires, needs, financial means, and abilities, so you can narrow down the myriad choices available to you. And after you've made your purchase, *Your New Sailboat* shows you how to maintain your sailboat in "Bristol fashion" for maximum resale value.

Your New Sailboat comes with the accuracy and authority that have become synonymous with *Chapman Piloting,* the premier name in marine publishing and the textbook used by the U.S. Coast Guard Auxiliary for all of its public sailing-education classes. You'll find detailed descriptions of sailboats of all makes, sizes, and construction. In addition, there's advice from the experts on everything from when to use a surveyor to stocking a galley to choosing the right anchor. You'll also find all the safety procedures you're required to follow as prescribed by the U.S. Coast Guard.

Handy charts, checklists, and diagrams in each chapter make sailing information accessible at a glance and allow you to develop your own customized maintenance schedules and safety checklists. You'll also find helpful Web site addresses and phone numbers for boating manufacturers and sailing organizations. Tips throughout offer special insights and some common-sense wisdom from experienced sailors.

This book isn't just a how-to book for boat buying, nor is it just about the mechanics of owning and safely operating a sailboat. It's about *sailing*: sailing as part of your lifestyle; what you can do with the boat after it's yours; how to use it responsibly while having the most fun with it. It will teach you to be a better sailor by building upon the expertise you already have. If you've been dreaming of a sailboat for family fun, single-handed sailing, racing, or cruising, all the information you need is right here in these pages.

Contributors to this book include Diana B. Jessie, Jim Jessie, and Ruth Ashby. Special thanks to Roger Marshall, yacht designer, veteran sailor, author, and Technical Editor with *Soundings*. Others who supplied valuable information are Dauntless Marina (Essex, CT), Sheila and Bob Gunther; John Ball; and Leslie Quarrier, yacht broker (Old Lyme, CT).

Note: All price ranges cited are as of 2002.

TABLE OF CONTENTS

PART I

THE DREAM...

For most people, buying a boat means realizing a dream. A boat can be a new hobby or the key to a whole different lifestyle. But once you've made the decision to buy, the excitement of prospective ownership can sometimes obscure more practical considerations. By asking yourself the right questions, you'll find the boat that's perfect for you. And that's the boat that guarantees the best sailing experience for you.

CHAPTER 1

ASK YOURSELF...

A boat represents a major investment of time, energy, and money—maybe the biggest one you'll make besides your home. So, treat it like any other major investment and do research before you commit. The best place to start is by asking yourself: **How am I going to use my boat?**

⚓ **TIP**

Call the U.S. Sailing Association (401-683-0800) or the American Sailing Association (310-822-7171) for lists of sailing schools nationwide.

Do you want your boat for use as a family activity? That's the most popular reason for owning a sailboat. Many families take the family cruiser away for weekends and vacations. Boating allows you to explore new places and meet new people; to learn, as a family, to be independent; and to enjoy the water and open air. If this is your goal, make sure that the whole family shares your enthusiasm, or else you may be in for some real disappointment. **Do you want to race or sail long distances?** Both require experience, special training, and equipment. **Do you want to live on your boat?** Even in the cold north, some people do so year round. But keep in mind that some states are legislating against live-aboard boaters, so you need to investigate your location of choice before deciding to live onboard.

If you don't have a concrete idea of what you want to do with your boat, but you have always had a dream of owning a sailboat, you're not ready to buy just yet. Take a **sailing course** or a **sailing school vacation** instead. Check with your local yacht club for information on sailing courses and schools, or look in the Yellow Pages or the back of any sailing magazine (or its website). That way, you can assess your skill level and later match it to the right type of boat.

If you want to learn to **race boats,** you might want to take a racing class at a sailing school. You should start out on a smaller boat to gain experience. After completing a course or two, going racing is a matter of getting to know people who race (at your local club or racers' hangout), and getting yourself invited along. Once you have established a good reputation, you will be asked to go racing a lot.

The Number 1 Question: Budget

Owning a large boat may be more expensive than owning a summer cabin. Sails, repairs, provisioning, dockage and haulouts are things that don't figure into the cost of a vacation home. But then again, you can't take your summer cabin to a new place every weekend.

What can you get for your money?

Cost is directly related to how you plan to use your boat and where you keep it. **Do you want to sail on a small lake?** Then your boat will be less expensive than (and not as large as) one you sail in coastal waters, in the Great Lakes, or on the open ocean. While a boat's cost generally reflects its size, it may also reflect the quality and reputation of the builder. For example, a 24-foot Hunter Marine pocket cruiser, a small boat capable of cruising in sheltered waters, may be relatively affordable, but a new J/24, a popular one-design racing boat, fully tricked out and ready to race, could cost twice as much. **Do you want to buy a new or a used boat?** Generally, you get more bang for your buck by buying a used boat. For example, a new 44-foot Nautor Swan, a top-of-the-line offshore cruiser/racer built in Finland, can cost upwards of $500,000, but a used model can be purchased for about $170,000. Your boat budget will have a number of components. By breaking them down and examining each one, you'll get an idea of the real costs of owning a boat. Let's start with the actual purchase price.

> **⚓ T I P**
>
> Whatever first boat you buy, you might want to think of it as the first in a series of upgrades. It may be wiser to spend a little less initially and discover what features are most important to you.

Can it be...less than $5,000?

You'll be limited to dinghies and other small boats less than 14 feet in length. For example, a new Optimist dinghy (or Opti), specially made for young sailors, costs about $2,500 to $3,000. On the other hand, a used Opti sells for between $1,500 to $2,750. A larger used dinghy in top-notch condition can cost up to $4,000. Be aware that you'll get only the basics: the boat and a sail.

Between $5,000 and $10,000?

For this price, you'll find a large selection of used boats up to 20-feet—good for lake sailing and in-shore cruising. You won't be able to sleep or cook on them, however. Bear in mind that these boats are generally no-frills. Being aboard will be more like camping out. Sailboats of this size (less than 8 feet in width) can be pulled by trailer, so you can take your boat anywhere and save in berth or storage fees. Your purchase price should include the cost of the trailer, but just to be safe, add the cost of the trailer (which will save money in berth or storage fees) to your budget calculations.

Between $10,000 and $25,000?

While you won't be able to afford a brand-new, race-ready J/24, you may be able to afford a used cruiser up to about 30 feet, built before 1985. Newer and larger boats will cost more. For a young family, a boat of around 30 feet will be ideal for coastal cruising and gaining experience.

> ⚓ **T I P**
> Typically, the older it is, the larger the boat you can buy for the same amount of money.

Between $25,000 and $50,000?

If you look carefully, you may find a boat up to 35 feet in this price range. And if you're willing to consider something as old as a 1978 model, you can probably buy a boat up to 38 feet. For example, both a 1992 Hunter 33.5 and a 38-foot 1976 C & C cutter sell for about $49,000. When looking in this range and above, don't exclude boats with an asking price of $55,000 or $60,000. You can always bid about 10 to 15% less.

Between $50,000 and $100,000?

With astute shopping, you can buy an older used boat up to 40 feet. For example, a 1981 Pearson 42 is available for around $79,000, but a brand new boat will be under 30 feet in this price range.

Between $100,000 and $200,000?

With this budget, you will be able to look at some new boats and many used boats. Some used 35-footers cost more than $140,000, while older 40-footers are available for close to the same price. With care, you could even find an older 50-footer such as a 1978 Gulf Star 50, a newer 43- to 45-footer such as a 1982 Mason 43, and a new 32- to 34-footer, all within this range.

Over $200,000?

The variety of available boats opens up tremendously at this price, with some good 50-footers being available. In this price range, it's prudent to consult a yacht broker.

Size not only affects price, it also determines how you can use a boat. Review the size options below and figure out which size best matches the type of sailing that interests you and the number of people you'll have aboard.

Can it be...14 feet or less (dinghies)?

Boats this small are not meant to be used on unprotected waters or after dark. They can accommodate only two or three people, and also capsize readily. So personal flotation gear must be worn whenever sailing. Racing dinghies typically have some form of flotation built into the boat. Even so, personal flotation is essential.

15 to 20 feet?

Boats in this range may be keelboats—boats with a keel under the hull instead of a centerboard, as is found on most small boats—and thus more stable. The smaller a boat is, the easier it is to transport. There are a few pocket cruisers in this size range with bunks, a stove, and a portable toilet, but most boats this size are intended for use in sheltered waters. Comfort and safety both dictate that no more than three people should be aboard at any one time.

21 to 26 feet?

These boats can have a number of uses. Some are classed as midget ocean racers. Boats in this size range have circumnavigated the globe by sailing from port to port. But from a practical point of view, there are limits to what you can expect. You won't be able to stand up inside the cabin. While some boats claim comfortable cruising for more than four people, this is true only if they are very compatible people. A racing boat in this size range usually has a crew of three or four who race during the day and sleep ashore at night (called day sailing or day racing).

> There is a transatlantic race called the **Mini-Transat** from France to the Caribbean for boats 21 feet or less. This race is for skilled sailors only who have well-found (or fully equipped) boats, which often cost upwards of $200,000.

TIP

If you're not sure how many hands will be on deck, get a boat that can be operated single-handedly. In a sailboat, this could mean a sloop that allows you to enjoy both single and short-handed cruising.

27 to 35 feet?

This is a great size for family cruising. Boats this big offer more interior space and comfort than smaller boats, and usually provide about six feet of headroom in the cabin. There are plenty of models on the market. Boats up to 35 feet can accommodate six to eight people for cruising. (But be prepared: you'll find that you'll live out of your seabag and that seabags fill almost all the available space when the bunks are in use.) You can sail a boat this size on lakes or on coastal or open waters, but you must use care when doing so. There are several popular one-design racing boats in this size range. Boats of this size are not easily transported by trailer, though, and are usually kept on a mooring or in a berth at a marina. In cold climates where ice forms on the water, these boats must be hauled out and stored on land during the winter.

36 to 50 feet?

Popular for ocean cruising, these boats are large enough to provide adequate storage space, headroom, and amenities and can accommodate up to ten people. Don't consider them for lake sailing, though (unless it's a Great Lake), because they require deeper water than many smaller boats. The size range works well for "liveaboards" because it can accommodate AC electricity, showers, and other necessities. Racing boats in this size range are usually custom-designed and are intended to be raced out of sight of land. Racing boats usually have a large number of bunks, but minimal head and galley layout. On a racing boat everything gives way to speed.

More than 50 feet?

Boats of this size are capable of going out into the ocean and being away from land for many days. Many are designed for cruising, while many are cruiser/racers, and some are designed solely for racing. Ocean cruising boats often use electronic autopilots and special sail features to cut down on crew. Racing boats usually accommodate eight to twelve people at any one time in order to have sufficient crew available 24 hours a day.

What's the water like? Where you live can limit your choices of where you sail, but keep in mind that some people drive for several hours to get to their boat and often use it as a second home. Others own a smaller boat and take it by trailer to different parts of the country to explore new places and scenery.

Do you want to sail on...a small lake or pond?

This type of sailing is widely appealing because it only requires a small boat. A small lake is an ideal location for learning or teaching sailing, but it limits the opportunities for experience with currents, waves, and navigation (be aware that sailing on a small body of water requires an excellent understanding of wind shifts and sail trimming). Lakes are popular venues for many small-boat racing fleets.

Coastal waters or the Great Lakes?

Sailing these waters offers the opportunity to experience a broader range of wind and water conditions. Likewise, these waters require a sturdier boat with protection from weather, storage space for gear, and more extensive safety gear. Knowledge of navigation is important, even if you are not out of sight of land. Most sailors navigate from buoy to buoy in these waters, although you should keep a running fix or dead-reckoning plot to ensure that you know where you are all the time. Sailing along the coast from harbor to harbor or between marinas is the most popular form of sailing, with lots of opportunities to make new friends.

Open ocean?

For these most challenging conditions, you'll need a well-constructed boat of a size that can be managed in a wide range of weather and sea conditions. Size is far from the only consideration. Crew compatibility, stamina, and the ability to cope with currents, waves, and variable wind conditions are also important factors. Because boats on the open ocean are likely to face storms, their design and construction should be adequate to withstand heavy weather. Most successful ocean sailors progress through a series of boats to find the right size, design, and sail plan for their needs.

Boats can be made of fiberglass, wood, metal, or ferro-cement. Each has its advantages and disadvantages. The following information should help you decide which type of construction best meets your needs. As you read, keep in mind that maintenance requirements vary depending on the construction material. See Part III for a detailed discussion of maintenance.

Fiberglass-hulled boats

Recreational production boats—boats that are made on a production line like cars and trucks—are made of fiberglass. It is readily available, fairly inexpensive, and requires less labor in the construction process than other materials. For the most part, fiberglass is durable and does not rot, and if it does require repair work or repainting, the work can be done easily by an amateur handyman. Fiberglass boats require less maintenance than do wood or metal boats.

Wooden-hulled boats

Older hulls of wood-plank construction can range in price from the relatively inexpensive to the very expensive. Wood requires expert care and maintenance, but its warmth and natural look often attract enthusiasts. Many wooden boats are beautiful under sail, and in the eyes of some sailors they are the only type of boat that should be on the water. Often a used wooden boat is quite inexpensive compared to a similar-sized fiberglass boat, but you'll need expert assistance to determine if a wooden boat is a good value. Furthermore, the extra maintenance can be costly. Wooden boats need to be carefully stored over the winter to avoid dry rot and are susceptible to marine borers. If you are interested in owning a wooden boat, it might be a good idea to take a course on reconstructing a wooden boat at a place like Mystic Seaport or the International Yacht Restoration School in Newport, RI.

> Because of increased air pollution, some **hulls** are being made using a vacuum-assisted resin transfer method (VARTM). It is cleaner and puts fewer volatile organic compounds (VOCs) into the atmosphere. The best known of these methods is SCRIMP (Seaman Composite Resin Infusion Manufacturing Process).

Steel boats

Steel boats are often heavily constructed. They are favored by cruisers who like to carry a lot of equipment. Because they have much more interior volume and weight, they tend to require a relatively large sail area and a larger-than-usual auxiliary engine. The advantages are more interior space and more equipment. The best steel boats are built in Europe; many in Holland. They are easy to handle, and the builders install reliable, efficient systems to eliminate standing water and use paints that withstand heavy usage and forestall the formation of rust. Whether or not the boat is European, it should be painted with high-quality marine paint specially developed for steel boats. A damaged steel hull can be repaired in just about any port in the world.

Aluminum boats

These are lighter than their steel cousins and cost about two-thirds more. Unlike steel, which rusts, aluminum oxidizes, which means that the outer layer of a freshly scratched aluminum boat reacts with oxygen in the air to form a protective layer. The result is that some aluminum-hulled racers that are thirty and forty years old still look like new.

Ferro-cement boats

These boats are usually inexpensive for good reason. The material is cheap, the labor is do-it-yourself, and even though all the other parts of the boat are similar to other vessels, ferro-cement boats do not hold their value because they are thought to be poorly made, hard to maintain, and very heavy. You may find a bargain in terms of size, but the integrity of construction must be examined carefully and resale may be next to impossible.

> **Custom boats** are built to an owner's specifications. This method of construction can make a boat about 20% more expensive than a production boat. Buyers of custom boats usually have a lot of boating experience and are looking for things not available in the production boat market. Custom boats may also have high-tech materials such as Kevlar or carbon fiber built into the laminate instead of fiberglass. Usually they are made with Vinylester or epoxy resin instead of polyester resins to make them stronger, lighter, and more impervious to osmosis problems.

TIP

To keep these boats in tip-top shape, care must be taken to eliminate sources of stray electrical currents that can turn an aluminum alloy boat into Swiss cheese when lying alongside a steel bulkhead. Provided you do this, there is no reason why an alloy boat should not last a long time.

The size and type of your boat and your budget will influence your decision in this area.

Small boats

A really small dinghy such as an Optimist, Laser, or 420 can be carried on a roof rack on your car. All you need to do is find a place to launch it. A small boat (up to about 28 feet) with a daggerboard or lifting keel (which can go up and down, as distinct from centerboards, which tend to pivot on a pin toward the front of the boat) is ideal for day sailing. It can be kept on a trailer in your driveway. Just be sure that you own or have access to a vehicle that is capable of towing a trailer—generally the size of an SUV or larger. For this type of boat, you may be able to use a municipal launching ramp or town dock, which will keep your costs low. But if that option is not available, you might have to pay to launch your boat at a privately-owned ramp or a hoist.

Larger boats

If the boat has a deep keel, as opposed to a centerboard or lifting keel, you may have to keep it in the water on a mooring (a floating buoy attached to an anchor chain, which is attached to an anchor or anchors). Or you may keep it on a trailer and launch it with a crane, paying to use the crane every time you launch. Boats over 30 feet must be kept in a marina or on a mooring. The advantage of a slip is that you can walk to your boat and step aboard. To get to a boat on a mooring, you will either have to row or motor out in your own dinghy, or get the yacht club or boatyard launch to take you out. There may be a charge for this service. Keep in mind that a boat on a mooring will require bottom painting, waxing, engine maintenance, provisioning, and cleaning every season. You'll have to do the work yourself or arrange for the boatyard to do it. In any case, these costs should be factored into your estimate. See Part III for more detailed information on maintenance.

Before buying a boat, it is essential to know where you will keep it and how much you can expect to spend on keeping it. You should arrange for the space before you take delivery. Typically, the larger the boat, the more difficult it is to find a space. Regardless of the size of your boat, it is likely that you will need to spend some money on this aspect of boat ownership. In northern areas you will also need to figure in the cost of winter storage.

Small boats

A boat that you can put on top of your car can easily live suspended from the roof of the garage or turned upside down on a platform in a yard or patio. Keeping a small boat at home involves little or no cost aside from the hardware for adapting the space.

Trailerable boats

Any trailerable boat can be kept in a driveway or parking area without cost, but some homeowners' associations have restrictions against this. If that's not an option, storage yards where RVs and similar vehicles are kept may offer places for trailerable boats. The cost of space in a storage yard or a boatyard varies depending on the area, the type of yard, and so on. If you have a boat with a fixed keel, it may be cost-efficient to store the boat in a boatyard with a small boat hoist, because the rate to use the hoist may be included in your space rental.

Moorings

Finding free, open water near the coast is rare. Just leaving your boat on its own anchor in a harbor is likely to cost you something. If the water is part of a municipality, there may be a fee. If you use a mooring buoy rather than your anchor, an annual or seasonal fee or rent will most likely be charged. In many parts of the country, there are mooring areas operated by clubs, government agencies, or private businesses in which moorings or dock space can be rented. Maintenance is usually provided by the business or club and additional to a membership fee, but in some cases, the boat owner is responsible. Usually there are restrictions on the size or weight of a boat permitted on a mooring. In any case, you will need transportation to get to your moored boat. Clubs often have a shore boat or tender to taxi their members between ship and shore. Other groups offer small rowboats to leave on your mooring or tow to a central dock. Alternatively, you might have to invest in your own rowboat or tender. This is an additional cost to consider.

Marinas

While tying up at a slip in a marina does away with the need for a shore boat, the cost is typically more than a mooring buoy and rowboat combined. The advantage is that the boat is in an area where it is protected from other boats and you can jump aboard whenever you wish. But be aware that marina space is often scarce. Some areas are so popular that there is a five- or six-year wait for a slip. Rents depend on the location, age, facilities, and size of the marina. Usually what you pay is calculated by the length of your boat on a monthly or seasonal basis. For example, if the rent is $10 per foot, and you have a 35-footer, this works out to about $3,500 per season (or more if you keep your boat in the water year round). If water and electricity are metered, then you will pay these charges as well. In some marinas, telephone installation and cable television are available for additional fees. If you want to live on a boat in a marina, there is often a surcharge for the privilege, and waiting lists are common.

Colder climates

In northern climates your boat will probably need to be hauled out for the winter and stored. You'll need to figure these fees into your overall budget as well. They can add $2,000 to $3,000 a year to boat costs. Add extra money if you plan to have the boatyard do work on your boat or winterize it.

Privately-owned docks

Owning a house on the water with a dock is a major expense. Keeping your boat at your own dock will also involve dock maintenance and insurance costs.

Boat ownership can be shared as a means of making your money go farther, but there are drawbacks, especially in terms of the availability of your boat. If you take on a partner or two, you will have to work out a reasonable plan for using the boat. An equitable plan requires tact and diplomacy. Before taking on a partner, it's a good idea to ask yourself if you are prepared to maintain the boat on your own if the partnership does not work out.

Bill-paying becomes more complicated in joint-ownership situations. Insurance companies and boatyards don't usually bill partners separately, and payments for berth rent, insurance, and haulouts must be timely. In partnership situations, it's best to set up a single fund for expenses such as gear replacement, repairs, and insurance. The catch is that someone has to be responsible for the fund. You should also make sure that all partners give equal attention to maintenance. Develop a check-sheet to make sure the boat is left ready for the next user, and schedule work days for partners to work on the boat together.

Time-shared or leased boats have the same issues as partnerships. If you invest your money in a joint-ownership situation and aren't satisfied with your access to the boat, rethink going solo.

Boat maintenance costs vary greatly based on size, age, and material. A small wooden dinghy that you can sand and paint without help will take some time and a few dollars for paint. A classic wooden schooner built in the 1920s or 1930s will require time, patience, and money. With this type of boat you can expect to pay about 10 to 15% of the boat's cost per year in maintenance. A new fiberglass boat will probably cost about 3% of its value in maintenance per year; an older fiberglass boat, about 10% of its value. Any boat that is kept in the water year-round should be hauled out annually for inspection and bottom paint. Fiberglass is popular because it requires less maintenance than a comparable wooden boat, but it will still need regular inspections and painting. And be aware that fiberglass boats built before 1986 and kept in the water year round can develop blisters—an expensive problem to solve.

Sails are expensive. Some people try to make their own, but it is usually not worth the effort. A suit of new sails will cost about 20 to 30% of the boat's value. Learning to take care of sails and performing preventive maintenance is the best way to reduce the cost. If you plan to be a competitive racer, sails are a major expense that you will need to budget annually. (See Chapter 7 for more information on sails.)

Outboard engines need to be flushed with fresh water at the end of the sailing season. Auxiliary engines also require regular maintenance and generally cost more for service and repair. It is important to have a regular service plan for your boat engine, just as you would for your car. (See Chapter 11 for more information on maintenance plans.)

TIP
How much can you do? Assess your knowledge of sailing and mechanical skills. See pages 27 to 31.

For smaller boats under 22 feet, **insurance** is typically written as part of homeowner's insurance. With most large companies, you can add a small boat to your policy based on a bill of sale and list of equipment. If you plan to trailer a boat, it's a good idea to check with your auto insurance agent first. For larger boats, you will need to deal with a specialist in marine insurance.

For some new boats and all used boats, regardless of size, insurors require a marine survey. In addition to paying the insurance premium, you pay the cost of the survey. However, the survey can then be used for other purposes, such as financing. Insurance premiums vary depending upon the value of the boat and where you plan to sail. (If you plan to sail to foreign countries, investigate insurance costs carefully.) Check the marina where you expect to keep your boat; it may require a special liability policy.

Most banks and loan companies offer boat **financing**, and there are other companies that specialize in marine loans. When you apply for the loan, don't forget to include sails, electronics, and other gear in the purchase price. If you don't, the loan amount might not be sufficient to cover all your costs. There are "blue books" for used boats, the two major ones being the NADA Marine Appraisal Guide and the BUC used boat guide. The loan officer will use the values quoted in these books and the marine survey to evaluate your loan. Check several sources to find the best financing.

Boats can be subject to a variety of **taxes**. Larger boats may be taxed as personal property or be subject to a use tax. Most states also have some form of sales or excise tax levied by the state or local government. With large boats, it is often the practice to purchase and register boats in states with lower or no taxes. However, the practice of registering your boat in one place and using it in another could present problems. For example, in Connecticut you're liable for sales tax on the value of your boat if you use it there for an extended period even if you've registered it in another state where there is no sales tax.

TIP
Check with the appropriate state department to find out about boat registration and licensing requirements. Usually, boats equipped with motors must be registered.

I t isn't for nothing that boats have been described as holes in the water into which you throw money. Unfortunately, there are many costs associated with boat ownership. In colder climates boats need to be stored for the winter, they need to be insured both in and out of the water, and every time the boat goes into or out of the water your boatyard will want to lighten your pocket. Here are some of the things you will want to consider:

Survey

Before you buy any sailboat over 18 feet long, get it surveyed. Most surveyors are competent professionals and can find things you may not have noticed. They will usually give you a list of work to be done either before or after you have purchased the boat. This list can be used to negotiate the price of the boat. In fact, a marine surveyor will probably save you more money than the survey fee by enabling you to negotiate the boat's price.

Registration

Most states require boat owners to carry a license and registration. Check your state's website or call the appropriate state department. (In some states this is the department of motor vehicles; in others the taxation department; while still others have the department under the environmental agency.) Boats equipped with motors are usually required to be registered, and in some states, the operator must have a boat-driving license.

Larger boats and boats that visit other countries are usually documented with the U.S. Coast Guard (USCG). This is usually done through a documentation broker and is in lieu of local registration, but check your own situation carefully. Ask your yacht broker how to get your boat documented if it is over 40 feet or will go out of the country.

Storage

In locales where the water freezes, you will need a winter storage space. If you can keep a boat in your garage or back yard, the only cost may be the hardware for adapting space. Winter storage in a boatyard can be expensive. Whether you pay an annual fee for a mooring of $50 per foot per year or a monthly rent in a marina, you need to know the year-round cost of keeping the boat before you buy it. This means that you need to figure in winter storage costs.

Fuel

If you are planning on buying a large cruising boat with a big engine and continuously running generator, add fuel expenditures into your budget. Remember that the cost of fuel in foreign countries may be double what you normally pay.

What's your weather like?

Will the climate where you live let you use your boat year round? Unfortunately, most people north of the Mason-Dixon line will answer "No." In this area people go boating from Memorial Day to Labor Day or late September, and then the boat is hauled out. But if you keep your boat in the water later than Labor Day in the north, you can get some wonderful fall cruises—especially to places like New York's Hudson River, where the fall foliage north of New York City is spectacular.

South of the Mason-Dixon line the season is longer, but your boat will still have to be hauled out for a short period. In Florida and southern California, your boat can be kept in the water year round.

In the colder north, you will spend from $1,000 to $3,000 per year, at a minimum, in winter storage and decommissioning costs, depending on boat size. If you have the yard do jobs such as winterizing your engines, draining water tanks, and covering your boat, these costs could easily rise to $10,000. In Florida, you will not have winter storage and decommissioning expenses, but you will have the cost of keeping your boat in the water, plus an annual haulout and bottom painting.

Any boat that is kept in the water should be hauled out annually for inspection and bottom paint. Fiberglass needs regular inspections and after ten to twelve years it may need base-coat painting. Fiberglass boats that were built prior to 1980 using polyester resins can develop blisters, if left in the water year-round. Depending on its severity, this problem can be expensive to solve. Engine maintenance is also essential and expensive.

Outboard engines will need to checked regularly. If they are used in saltwater, they need to be flushed at the end of each season with fresh water. On outboards, the bottom-unit oil will need to be changed and the cylinders misted before the engine is put away. Inboard engines require regular oil and filter changes (during the season if you run your engines hard; at the end if the season for moderate use). At the end of the season you'll need to have a competent mechanic go over the engine to check hoses, wiring, and belts, but if the engine is looked after well you'll have little trouble. At the end of the season you will need to winterize the engine by changing the crankcase oil and filters, draining the freshwater coolant, flushing the seawater coolant lines, and generally greasing and cleaning up the engine. Typically, this service at the beginning and end of each season puts the engine in good shape for the entire sailing season. Other than running out of fuel, most engines have few problems over the course of the season.

The Next Question: How Skilled Are You?

The next few questions will help you review your own skill level as well as the skills of people who will sail with you. Don't forget them: if your whole family expects to participate, be sure everyone agrees upon the kind of sailing you expect to do. Continually improving your skills will increase your confidence and enjoyment.

One way to start assessing your sailing skills is to estimate the amount of time you've spent on sailboats. If it's **a week or less,** take some courses before buying. You can take a course with a sailing school, at a municipal or yacht club program, or at any vacation sailing programs. With about a month's experience, you will have enough skill to handle a small boat, but you shouldn't stray too far from shore until you hone your skills a little more. At **two to three months,** you can have some real fun as long as you realize your limits. If you've sailed on other people's boats for **two or three seasons,** you've probably learned a lot. There's no reason not to own a boat, but plan offshore forays carefully. At **five years' experience,** you can buy any boat and go to most places. Once you've reached **ten years and more,** call yourself "Skipper." You can buy any boat and go wherever you want.

> **⚓ TIP**
> To gain sailing experience before you buy your own boat, offer to crew on other people's boats.

Of course, it's not just the amount of actual time you have spent on a boat. It's what you did that qualifies you to have your own boat. If you were just a passenger, take some courses before making any purchases. If you were indeed a member of the crew, and did something useful, think about buying a boat. If you were a crew on a boat going to Bermuda, you can buy a boat, but unless your experience is extensive, you shouldn't set off for Bermuda yourself right away. If your experience was as captain, you exercised ultimate responsibility for the boat and the people aboard and you can do it again. But until you are confident that you can be in charge of the boat and the lives of your family and any other people on the boat, take more experienced people along with you.

S ailing is athletic, so in addition to evaluating your sailing skills, you'll need to assess your fitness level. Dinghies and racing boats depend on muscle power. Agility and balance are essential in small boats that can be capsized easily. Even though all but the smallest sailboats will have auxiliary power in the form of an outboard motor or an installed engine, breakdowns on the water can and do occur. The better your sailing skills, the better able you'll be to get back to port.

Sailing Skills Checklist

Some specific sailing skills that are important to have:

- ► Overboard rescue
- ► Sailing to weather
- ► Sailing off the wind
- ► Tacking
- ► Jibing
- ► Reefing
- ► Docking under sail
- ► Anchoring
- ► Navigation

Overboard rescue This is the first and most important sailing skill. Start by insisting that sailors wear personal flotation devices. Sailboats need to be equipped with additional devices, including horseshoe rings, throwing lines, and retrieval devices. Of course, you must learn how to use the devices and practice using them with anyone who sails on your boat. Sailing schools and learn-to-sail textbooks provide specific information on overboard rescue procedures. See Chapter 12 for emergency procedures.

Sailing to weather This means you can efficiently sail a boat close to the direction from which the wind is coming. A boat usually heels (leans) when sailing to weather. With a dinghy, it is important to know at what angle heeling will become a capsize. Keel boats with flattish bottoms should not be allowed to heel more than about 20 degrees. If they go over further they become very slow. Deeply-veed hulls can be heeled to 25 degrees. Most boats will not capsize if they are allowed to heel. To stop the boat from heeling too far, simply let the sails out and then in (crank them back).

Sailing off the wind This term means you are sailing away from the direction of the wind. When the wind is directly behind you, it is called **downwind sailing.** Normally, sailing off the wind is more comfortable because the boat does not heel. Many sailors learn to sail off the wind more quickly than they learn to sail to weather. It's more comfortable for novices in your family, too.

Tacking means turning the boat's bow through the wind to change direction.

Jibing the boat means turning the stern through the wind to change direction. Both of these maneuvers are essential to learning to turn a sailboat.

Reefing refers to rolling or shortening a sail to make the sail area smaller. It's the maneuver used when the wind is too strong for a big sail. This is another skill you should learn on larger boats to help keep the boat upright. "Jiffy reefing" refers to a quick method of bringing areas of cloth onto the boom using a single line that runs through the sail tack (forward corner) along the boom and through the clew reefing eye (aft corner of the sail).

Learning to dock or pick up a mooring under sail is basic in small boat sailing. It is an important skill for owners of big boats in the event auxiliary power is lost. Docking **under sail or under power** requires practice because the direction of propeller rotation (prop torque) influences the direction a boat favors when turning and moving in reverse.

Anchoring is like using the parking brake in a car. All but the smallest boats, racing or cruising, will be equipped with an anchor to hold a boat to the seabed. Each boat behaves differently, so practice is important.

Navigation is essential to all sailing. It includes plotting a course, piloting from buoy to buoy or headland to headland, learning about tides and currents, and reading charts. Even small dinghies should have a compass for navigation. Larger boats have more gear for navigation depending upon where they are sailed. Recent advances in electronics have simplified the processes of determining your location on open water. See Chapter 9 for the latest in navigational advances.

You will acquire many other skills as part of sailing. With the basic steps behind you, you can progress in proficiency and independence at your own rate. The more skills you bring to owning your new boat, the more you will be able to enjoy it. As long as you're fit and can crank a winch handle, you can enjoy a lifetime of sailing. In later years, you can always invite younger, fitter people to sail with you and do the heavy chores, or you can buy a bigger boat with electric winches and roller furling gear and do everything at the push of a button.

YOUR SKILLS/ABILITIES

Mechanical skills are not essential, but they will lower the cost of boat ownership. Each task you can do for yourself gives you more confidence and independence. Even if a task is too large for you to accomplish alone, the fact that you can diagnose a problem yourself will make solving it easier.

Mechanical Skills Checklist

- ► Starting an outboard motor
- ► Repairing a pump
- ► Changing engine oil
- ► Checking a fan belt
- ► Assembling a winch
- ► Operating a sewing machine
- ► Surface prep and varnishing
- ► Unclogging a head
- ► Using compasses

Starting an outboard motor Outboards now come with electronic fuel injection and various other sophisticated electronics that make it easy to start and maintain them.

Repairing a pump There is a variety of pumps aboard larger boats. Pumps with diaphragms, impellors, or vanes are common. Learning to diagnose and repair pumps on your boat will save time and money. If you are unfamiliar with the types of pumps aboard your boat, get the mechanic at your local boatyard to show you the differences and how to repair them.

Changing engine oil This is a regular maintenance task with which you should be familiar. It can be messy, and depending upon the type of engine you have, the oil sump drain plug may be difficult to reach.

Checking a fan belt Checking fan belt tension is relatively easy—you simply press on the belt. If it sags about 3/8" to 5/8" it's OK. More than that, and you'll have to adjust the idler pulley to retension the belt. Seeing a build-up of belt dust under the fan belt is a sign that things are misaligned.

Assembling a winch Most sailboats have winches to gain mechanical advantage when hoisting and trimming sails. Winches must be cleaned and lubricated regularly. Taking a one-speed winch apart and putting it together is difficult the first time but gets easier with practice. Taking apart a two- or three-speed winch should only be done with the manual and spares kit next to you. If you can put a three-speed winch with backwind back together without having it revolve the wrong way, you can probably get a job with a winch manufacturer.

Operating a sewing machine This is an important skill if you intend to cruise long distances away from shore facilities. Repairing canvas covers and cushions with a machine is quick and very cost effective. Some sails can be repaired on your boat with a sewing machine, but those repairs should be viewed as temporary until you can go to your local sailmaker.

Surface prep and varnishing The charm of many boats is in the wooden trim used to finish the interior and exterior. This wood is referred to as brightwork. Learning to sand and varnish your brightwork without brush marks requires patience but rewards you with a well-kept look to your boat. Many owners enjoy this task and find it therapeutic.

Unclogging a head "Head" is the term for a marine toilet. Unclogging one is an unpleasant task. If you make sure that they are used properly, there is less likelihood of having to undertake it. However, if you have children with small toys you will do it at least once. Taking it apart and cleaning it is a skill that will save you time and money, but this is a task you might want to spend money on and let the yard do it.

Using compasses Knowing how to use compasses correctly is essential for navigation. Compasses respond to magnetic influences and can register incorrectly. Swing your compass (adjust it to your locale) before you head out to sea on your first trip. Hire an expert to do this job for you if you are at all unsure. And never place any ferrous objects near the compass.

Single-handed

If you want to sail alone, remember that you are totally responsible for yourself and your boat. You must be capable of handling the boat in all situations. Racing a small dinghy alone is not so demanding because there is usually a rescue boat nearby, but sailing a boat around the world alone is another story. Personal flotation devices (PFDs), safety gear, electronic beacons, and a life raft are important, but most important is your ability to survive.

With others

If you want to take family or friends on a special outing, be sure one of them is an experienced sailor. If not, invite one. The safest course is to always have more than one experienced sailor on board. Even so, plan to restrict your sailing to protected waters and only tackle short distances. Before you leave the dock or launching pier, have everyone put on a PFD.

Taking children on a boat adds to your responsibility as captain. Young children should wear PFDs on board and even when they are on the docks around boats. Knowing how to swim is important, but an unconscious child cannot swim, so keep those PFDs on. If you plan to cruise as a family, your children should learn sailing skills and become responsible crewmembers.

TIP

Taking an extra person on an overnight trip requires more than just another berth. It means more capacity for storage, food, water, and washing!

Many **people with disabilities** are able to participate in sailing activities. Boats can be modified to increase mobility or limit the amount of physical strength required for particular tasks. A more difficult issue is the lack of balance or stability a disabled person might feel on a sailboat. Many disabled people can go on a day sail on a small boat with no problems. Overnight passages and spending a night on an anchor are more challenging. Racing presents more unpredictable situations than does cruising. Tasks that fall to the disabled person must be manageable regardless of weather conditions or gear failure. Keep these eventualities in mind when you practice. If you have a disability or plan to sail regularly with someone who does, plan to modify the boat with additions such as swivel seats, ramps, and motorized stairs. Shake-a-Leg, based in Newport, RI, is an organization for disabled sailors that can help with ideas.

Pets onboard

Many people with cruising boats wouldn't think of sailing without the family pet, but having a pet aboard takes careful planning. You need to think about food, water, and some toilet facility, even for daysailing. For long trips, animals need to be trained to use litter boxes or a designated area. It is usually difficult for dogs to manage on a sailboat because they don't have a way to grip the deck when the boat heels. Cats can adapt by holding on with their claws. Flotation for pets is advisable, particularly if there are heavy seas. Also bear in mind that getting a dog or other pet ashore is often difficult. If you want to leave your boat and visit on land, rules governing whether your animal may come ashore vary from place to place.

TIP

Keep your pets safe! Before you bring a pet aboard, get him his own personal PFD. The smallest pet vests also fit cats.

▲ **A safety harness ensures that you know where your**
child **is at all times aboard a boat.**

Many new owners believe they will spend all of their time on their new boat. However, the length of time spent on a boat often reflects how the boat is used. If you are not sure what you want to do with it when buying a boat, ask other boat owners how often they use their boats, what they do with them, and how they organize their time. This information may directly influence what you buy.

Racing boats

Racing boats tend to be used mainly for short periods. Races have specific start times and limits on finishing times. One-design boats, identical sister ships from the same mold, may spend an afternoon racing a ten-mile course or an entire day racing ten or twenty miles. Because racing is planned, use of a racing boat is more organized and specific than cruising.

Racing boats can be small (for low-budget operators); one-design, handicap racers (for owners who want to spend a lot of money getting their boats to go fast); or ocean racers (for owners who want to disappear over the horizon, only to reappear in three days in need of a shave, a shower, and decent food).

Cruising

Cruising suggests a relaxed lifestyle. If you are happy with a small cruiser and trailering, you can enjoy cruising without huge initial costs or upkeep. As you expand your cruising horizons, you will spend more on amenities and a bigger boat that can accommodate them. On a bigger boat that is capable of going farther, you could easily spend an entire weekend. Your use may be every weekend during the summer, or several weekends plus your vacation time.

TIP
If you plan to cruise for longer than a day with other adults, plan on at least one semi-private area per person or couple.

Live aboard

Of all the things you can do with a sailboat, living on one is probably the most satisfying and many are designed for that purpose. If you want a boat that you can sail and live on at the same time, you will either have to have a big boat or do without some amenities. Most people who move aboard do so to simplify their lives. Living aboard a boat means that you will accumulate a lot of gear that makes for slow going. Cruising long distances, even around the world, is a goal that will cost money to attain, but it has rewards that will satisfy you for the rest of your life.

Are you a creature of comfort?

The comfort level you expect will be a big factor in deciding what type of boat to buy.

If you expect to be dry, warm and comfortable, sit on deck and read, use a toilet, take a shower, and have hot meals and a comfortable bunk, you might buy a boat over 32 feet. Dinghies and open boats don't have toilets, so you may be faced with using a bucket, leaping over the side, or waiting until you get to land to obey the call of nature. In general, the larger the cruising boat, the greater the creature comforts.

If you decide to go ocean racing, your creature comforts will be minimal. You will wear flotation gear and maybe a harness. If you go on an offshore race, you may share a spartan bunk with someone else (known as hot-bunking), eat food direct from a hot can or pouch, and use a head protected only by a curtain.

> **⚓ TIP**
> If you know you will have small children on board, look for a boat with a deep cockpit, comfortable seating, shade, and a marine head.

The conventional wisdom is that you don't really need power for anything under 15 feet and you can row or scull a boat up to 24 feet long quite easily. Many French sailors use a single long oar over the transom to scull their boats for long distances. However, anyone who has been becalmed for an afternoon might argue for at least an auxiliary engine.

For boats under about 28 feet, gas-powered outboards, either two- or four-cycle, are the most common type of engine. Outboards are usually fitted on a bracket that will swing up when the boat is under sail and hinge down when needed to power the boat. Very few boats have a gas inboard. They have a nasty habit of collecting gasoline fumes in the bilge and can explode.

A diesel inboard is the most popular type of engine on sailboats above 28 feet. Diesels come in a wide range of sizes. Choose a size that is adequate to power the boat and to support additional generators or alternators and pumps installed on the engine. Diesels tend to have lower fuel costs but cost slightly more than a gas motor initially. If you have a diesel inboard on a sailboat, you may have one of three types of propeller: a fixed-blade prop, one where blades fold flat to reduce hydrodynamic resistance (folding type), or one with flat blades (feathering type) that fold fore and aft for least resistance. For racing and best sailing performance the feathering prop is best, with the folding prop a close second. Both sometimes fail to open properly when the engine is switched from ahead to astern rapidly. If you intend to power your boat a lot, a fixed-blade prop is the most efficient. Most larger boats come with an engine. You should only change it if the existing engine is worn out or doesn't have enough power to push the boat.

How much time will you spend maintaining your boat?

Maintenance requires budgeting both time and money. Whether or not you do the work yourself, purchase at least one good book on boat maintenance so that you have some idea of the scope of what is involved. Cruising boats do not require much maintenance, but you should allow at least one day of maintenance for each week of sailing. That may seem like a lot, but most of the maintenance can be done when the boat is hauled out and sitting in winter storage.

In northern climes the boat will have to be hauled out at the end of the season, decommissioned, and made ready for winter. Over the winter, a major portion of the maintenance can be completed. But leaving all maintenance until you haul the boat out is not a good plan unless you have kept a meticulous record of what needs to be done and included it in the winter work list. If you do not have a record, you will most likely forget what should be done and still have problems next season. Also, it will be too cold to complete chores such as varnishing, polishing, and on-deck maintenance. Save these jobs for spring.

If you keep your boat in the water year round, it will still have to be hauled out once a year. Before it comes out of the water, you should have a good idea of what work needs to be done and have any necessary supplies (paint, rollers, etc.) ready. You should also plan to do smaller chores while the boat is afloat. Varnishing, painting, and cleaning can easily be done on a sunny afternoon with the boat in the water. If you visit your boat regularly to clean, organize, replace parts, and paint or polish, you are more likely to discover problems before they become major, and your boat will remain in tip-top shape. If you only work on the boat the day you use it, chances are that you will be in a hurry, miss something important, or be rushed and fail to recognize the symptoms of a problem.

Keep a **maintenance log** of breakages, jobs that need doing, and anything else that should be done on the boat at periodic intervals. This maintenance log helps to demonstrate that the boat has been kept up properly when you are ready to sell it again, and also ensures that you keep up with the work that needs doing.

CHAPTER 2

WINDOW SHOPPING

Having addressed the questions in Chapter 1, you have a much better idea of what you want in a sailboat: what you can afford, and what your skills and mechanical abilities are. Now it's time to get more specific. You know approximately what you want a boat for, and what types of boat might fit your needs. Before you take any further steps, you should learn as much as you can about sailboats.

About Sailboats

Not all sailboats are alike, but every sailboat can be propelled by wind and sails. Most sailboats over 18 feet long also have an engine. Boats over 28 feet usually have an inboard diesel auxiliary engine. Small, open sailboats are usually called daysailers, and those used primarily for racing may be known as racing dinghies, although the word "dinghy" is usually reserved for a very small boat used to ferry crew and supplies.

A motorized dinghy is called a **tender.** Boats with more than one hull are known collectively as **multihulls.** There are two major types of multihulls: **catamarans** and **trimarans.** Catamarans have two hulls that are either identical or mirror images of each other. Trimarans have three hulls: a larger central hull for crew accommodation and two smaller outer hulls that also may have accommodations in them.

A sailboat may have a **cockpit** near the front or back, or in the middle of the hull. Because a cruising sailboat cockpit is both an entertainment and a control center, compromises must be made between access to lines to hoist and trim sails (halyards and sheets) or to devices to increase the pull on such lines (winches) and the comfort of the crew. Typical cockpits have facing bench seats that are close enough together so that crew members can brace themselves as the boat heels. Cockpit seats sometimes open to reveal seat lockers and stowage facilities.

On newer boats, aft cockpits tend to be shallower and open to the sea. This feature allows the boat to shed water quickly if the cockpit gets flooded, and also allows additional space inside the hull under the cockpit for a double berth on a cruising boat.

On center-cockpit boats the engine compartment is usually directly under the cockpit. Ladders lead both forward and aft to allow access to the hull interior. Often there is a passageway from the forward accommodations to the aft cabin, as well as a ladder.

A **pedestal** with a steering wheel may stand near the aft end of the cockpit. On top of the pedestal is a **compass**. The pedestal may also support shift and throttle controls for the auxiliary engine. The wheel controls the rudder that steers the boat. On sailboats up to about 30 feet, a **tiller** (a handle attached to the top of the rudder post) replaces and serves the same function as the wheel.

Whether a boat uses a wheel or a tiller, the steering controls are called the **helm**. The person handling those controls is called the helmsman. The cockpit and the main cabin are connected by a companionway consisting of a steep set of ladder-like steps, grab rails, and a sliding hatch. The part of an aft cockpit that must be stepped over at the top of the companionway is called a coaming or bridge deck, and is an important safety feature. If the cockpit were to fill with water from a large wave, the coaming or bridge deck would keep the water from going down into the interior and collecting in the bilge (the space under the cabin sole boards).

TIP

Do you like to go fast—*really* fast? Check out a sailboard—a surfboard with a sail. And expect to get wet!

SAIL PLANS

Sailboats are usually known by their sail plans: the number of masts and the position of their sails.

The Sloop

The most popular sail plan is the sloop, which has a single mast with a mainsail and a headsail. The forward sail is the jib (if it does not overlap the mast) or genoa (if it overlaps the mast) and the aft one is the mainsail, also called the main. A sail's leading edge is its luff; its after edge is the leech, and the bottom edge is the foot. A triangular sail's upper corner is called the head. The aft corner is the clew and the forward bottom corner is the tack. Years ago a jib was attached to the headstay with hanks, strong hooks with spring-loaded closures, but today most boats use a headfoil with roller furling gear.

Headsails can have many names, depending on their size, weight, and shape. The smallest is a storm jib, followed by a heavy-weather jib and then a working jib. In general, sails are referred to as a percentage of their length from the headstay to the forward edge of the mast. This distance is known as the J. and the largest is usually 150% of J.

The Cutter

A single-masted sailboat similar to the sloop, the cutter has its mast slightly further back, leaving room for a larger fore-triangle filled by two headsails. The upper headsail is the jib, while the lower is a staysail. If the cutter has a bowsprit, a third sail, or flying jib, may be fitted at the end of the bowsprit. A cutter rig has two advantages. First, it divides sail area among smaller sails that are more easily handled. Second, it provides more sail reduction options in rough going than does a sloop. And when the sail is furled, the remaining sail area is closer to the mast, giving added safety in a seaway. This rig has been a longtime favorite among cruising sailors who like a single-mast rig.

The Ketch and the Yawl

The ketch and yawl look somewhat alike. Both have a tall mainmast and a shorter mizzenmast (smaller mast aft of the mainmast) that flies a mizzen sail. The distinction between a ketch and a yawl is a common topic of debate among sailors. Traditionally, the governing rule is the location of the mizzenmast: if it is ahead of the rudder post, the boat is a ketch; if it is behind the rudder post, the boat is a yawl.

Ketches and yawls are divided rigs, meaning the sail area is divided between two masts. Either craft may have a masthead or a fractional rig forward of the mainmast. Individual sails are more easily handled by a small crew. On a reach, both rigs may add an extra sail between the masts, such as a mizzen staysail. Because of the extra rigging and mast surface area exposed to the wind, these rigs have more windage and are less effective on smaller boats where windage is relatively more important. The ketch and yawl rigs are popular among cruising sailors for long-distance voyages. Mizzenmasts have a practical location for mounting electronic antennas (such as radar or VHF).

The Schooner

The schooner is a vessel with at least two masts (in the last century, some carried up to seven). On two-masted schooners, the mainmast is aft and is at least as tall as or taller than the forward mast, or foremast. The modern schooner rig may carry a jib-headed main and foresails that are triangular (like the mainsail on a sloop). The foresail may be loose-footed— not fitted with a boom—and there may be only one headsail.

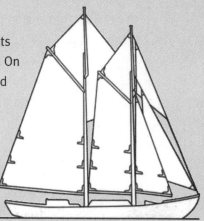

Schooners are at their best in steady trade winds on long ocean passages. Although they do not sail to windward as well as other rigs, they make up for it when the wind is on or aft of the beam.

The Catboat

A boat that features only one mast set far forward and only a mainsail is known as a catboat. Traditionally, these have been small, inshore boats. (Lack of redundancy in the rig was an issue when rigs were considerably less reliable.) The catboat was a very useful and practical design for coastal fishermen because there was less rigging to get in the way when handling nets on the water or unloading the catch ashore. Also, the boat's single sail was easier for one person to handle.

Recent cat-rigged designs make use of unstayed masts (masts that have no standing rigging, but are supported only by the deck). With less

windage and high, narrow sail plans, modern catboats often can perform as well as sloop rigs. Because the sail plan is based on a mast well forward in the boat, cat rigs tend to have lots of weather helm.

Types of sailboats

Below is a short list of sailboat manufacturers. Most of them have Web sites—check them out.

Dinghies—one person

▶ Laser, Laser II, Pico, Laser Radial, Optimist, Pram, Sunfish, Zuma (www.teamvanguard.com)

▶ El Toro (www.eltoroyra.org)

▶ Sabot, Wave (www.catalinayachts.com)

Dinghies—two people

▶ Flying Junior

▶ Pelican

▶ 420, 29er, 49er, Vector, Vanguard 15 (www.teamvanguard.com)

▶ Coronado, Expedition, 12.5, 13, 16.5 (www.catalinayachts.com)

Multihull—open

▶ Hobie Cat

▶ Escape (www.escapesail.com)

Daysailer (under 30 feet)

▶ Alerion (www.proper-yachts.com)

▶ Aero 20, Catalina 16, 18, Johnson 18, Independence 20, Capri 22 (www.catalinayachts.com)

▶ Freedom Marshall Cats

▶ MacGregor

▶ Westwight Potter

Multihull Cruisers

▶ Endeavor Catamarans

▶ Corsair Trimaran (www.corsairtri.com)

▶ Fountaine Pajot

▶ Island Cat (www.islandcatamaran.com)

▶ Lagoon ▶ Packet Cats ▶ Privilege Cats

⚓ **T I P**

The Sunfish is a great board boat for kids 11 and older. They can sail it themselves—and even right it when it capsizes!

One-Design—racing

- Etchells ► Express 27
- Farr 40 ► IODs
- J/22 ► J/24
- Moore 224 ► Melges 30
- Shields

Coastal Cruisers

- Bavaria
- Beneteau (www.beneteauusa.com)
- Caliber
- Catalina 22, 250, 270, 28 Mk II, 30 Mk III, 310, 320, 34 Mk II, 380, 390 (www.catalinayachts.com)
- Dufour (www.DufourYachts.com)
- Hunter
- Jeaneau (www.JeanneauAmerica.com)
- Pacific Seacraft (www.pacificseacraft.com)
- Sabre Yachts (www.sabreyachts.com)
- Tartan

Offshore Cruisers (occasionally raced)

- Alden ► Baltic yachts
- C & C ► Halberg-Rassey
- Hinckley ► Island Packet
- J-Boats ► Moody
- Nautor Swan ► Oyster
- Santa Cruz 52 ► Taswell
- Valiant Yachts (www.valiantyachts.com)
- Wauquiez ► X-Yachts

Collecting Boat Information

You will want to collect as much information as you can on boats in which you think you might be interested. There are a number of sources—articles and advertisements in periodicals, the Web, or boat shows. Check your local library or bookstore for periodicals such as *Sail*, *Sailing*, *Sailing World*, and *Soundings*. They offer articles on sailing technique, different types of boats and equipment, and cruising. Even photographs of boats in advertisements can help you focus in on the boat you think might be right for you.

The Web has so much information that a good search engine can save you lots of time and running around. Most major sailboat makers have their own Web sites where you can look for more specific information about boats you're interested in. Check out the list of sites given above in "Types of Sailboats." If you know you're interested in a used boat, there are many sites that can make your search easier. There are also Web sites that list hundreds of used boats, such as:

▶ www.boattraderonline.com

▶ www.soundingsonline.com

▶ www.yachtworld.com

If you can, print out any pages you think you might want to refer to later. That way you'll have a home library for ready reference.

Another useful site is www.nadaguides.com, the NADA Appraisal Guide site. Although this doesn't offer lists of used boats, it does offer pricing information from the guide itself. If you want to see what's available in your area, go to the Web site of your local newspaper, where you can access the classified section. Depending on the newspaper, the classified ads may be updated every day or every week.

Boat shows provide most buyers with the best opportunities to make comparative decisions. Even if you are convinced that you will be buying a used boat, consider attending boat shows. If you want to "do" a show properly, start preparing before the show starts.

Start with the brochure:

- ► Look at the numbers first to get a feel for the boat. Is it the right length overall? The longer the waterline, the faster the boat will sail.
- ► Is the beam (width) adequate?
- ► Are the bunks carried into the ends of the boat (where the motion of the boat will be exaggerated)?
- ► Is the galley suitable for your type of cooking?
- ► Is the engine adequate? Remember: adding extras like a larger alternator or a bilge pump robs the engine of three to five horsepower.
- ► What type of keel is it? A deep keel keeps you out of a lot of harbors; a shallow keel may reduce stability.

After you have narrowed your list to six or eight boats, go to a boat show. If your schedule permits, choose a day when attendance is low, usually on the first "Red Carpet" days. Take along a notebook, a tape measure, and a camera. Take time and go over each boat you are interested in carefully.

Hop aboard and look the boat over. Use your tape measure because appearances can be deceiving. Check the length of the berths (they should be at least 6 feet 4 inches), check the berth widths (at least 28 inches). Check the dining table size and the table seating. Do you have enough seats for your sailing party? Do you have enough berths?

If you narrow it down to one or two boats, ask to make arrangements for a trial sail. While you spend a lot of time at a show looking at boats, don't forget that equipment matters, too. Equipment manufacturers may also be represented at the show, so visit them, too. See if they have newer or better equipment that may not be shown on the boats. If you come away feeling overwhelmed, you're not alone. Remember that your opinions may change quickly as you gain some experience, so don't plan to make a purchase decision based solely on a boat show encounter.

By doing this homework, you've been able to narrow your choices down considerably. So when you actually go out to shop, you can limit the number of boats you see to ten instead of thirty. If you are buying a small boat, you can go to a dealership and look at the range. (If you prefer not to run around from dealership to dealership, you can try shopping by phone.) A salesperson should be able to give you a lot of information in a relatively short period of time.

Here are some of the questions you will want to ask:

- ► What models do you have in stock?
- ► What options does the boat have that are not in the brochure?
- ► How much does the boat—on the water and ready to sail—cost?
- ► How does the boat handle in rough water?
- ► What's the standard hull warranty (if it is not in the brochure)?
- ► Can you have a trial sail or demo?

Most sailboats are not sold from a roadside dealership, but rather from a boatyard or a dealer with an office in a boatyard or marina. Typically, the dealer will have two or three models in the water ready for sailing, but may not have the model you want in stock. If this is the case, most dealers will send you to a yard or dealership that has a similar boat available for you to look at. This is why boat shows are so useful. At larger shows many manufacturers display their entire line of boats.

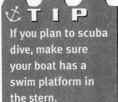

After you have made your decision, you will start discussing with the dealer what options are available, what colors you might want, what sail and rig combinations are best. You might go through the entire inventory of options one by one and end up buying everything ready to go afloat from the one dealer. If you want to save money, though, you may be better off getting the boat from the dealer and buying the extra equipment from your local chandlery or retail marine store. Often if you explain that you are fitting out an entire boat, you can get a quantity discount.

TIP

If you plan to scuba dive, make sure your boat has a swim platform in the stern.

Shopping for a Used Boat

The first step when looking over used boat ads is to decide on a budget. Generally, you can go 15% over your budget to bid on larger boats because you will usually bid low. For example, suppose you believe you have $65,000 to spend. In reality, you can look at boats up to $75,000. When you find the boat you want, you might decide to bid $60,000. The owner drops to $70,000 and you offer to split the difference, making the cost $65,000.

So now you are looking at boats with a value of about $75,000. How do you know what is good value for your money? The short answer is that you don't without doing a fair amount of homework. Boats don't all age or depreciate at the same rate. Some boats hold their value and drop only a few percentage points per year. The value of other boats plummets like a stone as soon as they leave the dealer's yard. The only way to determine whether a boat is a good deal is to get as much information as possible on the make and model number as you can find through Web sites and magazines. Then go through the list and see what boat is in the best shape for the best price, with the best gear. The highest-priced boat may be priced that way because it is rare in the part of the country where it is. The lowest-priced boat may be a wreck. Inspect as many boats as possible and figure out which one best suits you.

Finally, check out the resale prices of boats three years older than the one you intend to buy. If they are 25% lower than the boat you are about to buy, expect to lose about 25% when you resell this boat in three years. If the prices are only 5% lower, that boat might be a good deal.

Find out as much as you can from the boat's owner. Ask:

► Why are you selling the boat?

► How old is the boat? How long have you owned it?

► How long has the boat been for sale? Are you negotiating with anyone else?

► How much are you selling the boat for? Are you flexible on the price? How did you determine that price?

► What are the boat's major strengths? Major weaknesses?

► How quickly does the boat respond in light air and in heavy air?

► What kind of repair work have you done? Does the boat leak?

► Do you have the maintenance records?

If you are seriously interested in the boat, you should do a thorough inspection before proceeding any further (see Chapter 4). You might want to come prepared to do your own mini-inspection the first time you see the boat. In any event, bring your crew with you on your initial trip.

Using a broker

To buy anything over 30 feet, you should go to a yacht broker. It will make things much easier. A broker will ask you a lot of questions. In fact, your broker might ask all the questions outlined in Chapter 1. Armed with what your specific needs and desires are, brokers will search their databases for good matches. Most brokers belong to a multiple listing service that tells them about thousands of boats worldwide. The broker then suggests boats that are in your price range and desired style, and suitable for your needs.

Brokers save travel time, too. Say you live in Boston and a great deal comes up at the Valiant brokerage house on Lake Texoma, Texas. To check it out, you have to fly to Dallas-Ft. Worth, rent a car, and drive to Lake Texoma. If the deal is a bust, you've spent time and money for nothing. A broker simply checks in with the Valiant broker, who will have inspected the boat with an experienced eye and written a brokerage listing on it. For the price of a phone call, your broker has checked out the boat. Of course, you could call the Valiant broker and theoretically get the same answers, but brokers tend to talk more plainly with other brokers. If that deal is a bust, the broker simply moves on to the next boat until the right boat is found for you.

When you work through a broker, that broker works for you. He or she gets paid when you buy the boat. Typically, the seller pays the brokerage fee, so you don't spend any money. A selling broker gets between 8% and 10% of the selling price. If your broker does not have an exclusive listing on the boat, the fee is usually split equally between both brokers. If your broker works for a brokerage house, the fee will be split between the broker and the house. So, after putting in a lot of work, your broker may only end up with 2% to 2.5% of the selling price.

Since most brokers subscribe to a multiple-listing service, it's consequently a waste of time to go to multiple brokers to find the same information. It is far better that you find a broker you like. Who knows? This might be the professional you'll use to sell your boat when you're ready to upgrade.

CHAPTER 3

WHAT CAN YOU AFFORD?

L et's say you've done as much research as you can on sailboats. You know what you want to use the boat for. You know which boats you're interested in; you have an idea what they cost. Now comes the crucial question: **What can you afford?**

The Cost of a Sailboat

Financier J.P. Morgan once said about buying a boat, "If you have to ask how much it costs, you can't afford it." As a rich man, he knew he'd never have to ask the question of himself. Most of us aren't so privileged. We need to know exactly how much we're going to spend—and whether we can (or should) do it.

As with other important purchases in life, you need to consider not only the overall costs, but also how much you will spend on a monthly basis. It's also important to remember that most boats are not good investments. Unlike a house, boats usually do not appreciate in value over the years. It is harder to sell a used boat than a used house or car. So checking out the resale value of the boat that you are about to buy is important. At least you'll know what you're getting into.

So again—make sure you can afford it. It is better to start small than to start big. Most people tend to overestimate their purchasing power. If you have to err, make it on the side of frugality.

Price

When examining two boats of the same length, it is usually apparent why one is more expensive than the other. One boat may have a hull of ferro-cement, another of composite construction. Ferro-cement hulls generally sell for a lot less than a fiberglass boat of the same size, in spite of the fact that the engine, sails, and amenities are exactly the same. One sailboat may have a painted interior, another might be hand-polished teak. The quality and equipment aboard boats varies tremendously, as does the care and maintenance that boats get. Consequently you should be prepared to walk away from a bad deal for a more favorable one.

It is rarely necessary to pay the asking price for a new boat. Most new boats are marked up 20% to 30%, and the seller has some flexibility in agreeing to a fair price. Both sides compromise, and everyone can feel good about the final transaction.

> **TIP**
> If you are buying a trailerable boat, make sure the dealer gives you the price of the trailer up front. It can add $1,200 to $2,500 to the purchase price of a new boat.

Payments and Interest

Cash is best, but most people have to finance their boats for up to fifteen years. Financing makes it possible to enjoy your boat while you are paying for it. It also means that, with interest, you can end up paying almost twice the principle. The easiest way to estimate five-year payments at 8 to 10% is by multiplying the number of thousands by 20—that is, a $5,000 boat will have payments of around $100, a $10,000 boat will run around $200, and a $20,000 boat will cost around $400 per month. You can also get an accurate figure by going online to almost any brokerage house, bank, or boat listing service. Just enter figures for the principle, interest rate, and length of loan.

If you don't know what the prevailing interest rate is, call a bank to find out. Then figure out how much you can pay as a down payment. These two figures should give you a good idea how much you can pay for a boat. Another way to check this information is to go to a boating or banking website and check their tables of interest. Many financial and boating websites have a loan calculator where you put in the amount of the loan, the interest rate, and the length of the loan, and it will give you the monthly payment.

PAYMENTS ON A $50,000 BOAT AT 10% INTEREST		
Term	Monthly Payment	Interest Over Full Term
60 months	$1,062.35	$13,741.00
120 months	$660.75	$29,290.00
180 months	$537.30	$46,714.00

Depreciation

Depending on the builder, your new boat may immediately drop in value. Generally, the less expensive a boat is to buy new, the greater the depreciation will be. Very expensive, well-cared-for boats drop only a few percent from year to year, while others may drop 25%. Depreciation is nice when you are buying a used boat, but discouraging when you are paying off a 15-year loan. Just remember—the ultimate value of a boat lies in the enjoyment you get out of it, not the money you put into it. Nonetheless, the fact of depreciation is a very useful corrective when you are tempted to pay more than you can afford for a boat.

Sails

If you buy a used boat you may find that it comes with still-usable sails. Sails generally start to deteriorate within the first few months of use, and continue to deteriorate every time they are used. On racing boats, for which performance is carefully monitored, performance deteriorates after 100 hours or so. In the America's Cup, small sails decline in performance after 80 to 90 hours of sailing. Cruising boats can perform adequately with some performance deterioration. However, if the sails are more than two seasons old, you should think seriously about buying new ones.

Most new cruising boats come with a mainsail and at least one jib, but for top-of-the-line new boats you will need to buy your own. You can find out more about sails in Chapter 7. Sails are a big-ticket item. If, for instance, you have bought a 30-foot sloop, you will need at least one mainsail, at about $3,000 to $4,000; a roller-furled genoa, at about $3,300; and a staysail at $1,500. For offshore sailing, you will want to add storm sails and possibly a spinnaker—that is, if you have spinnaker gear. Sails and peripherals like a mainsail cover can easily cost you an additional $10,000.

> If you think your sails are tired, take a look at the **clew rings**, the stitching, and the seams. Distorted clew rings show that the sail has been stretched considerably. Delamination of the material and stretch marks around the corners show the same. Missing or torn seams show that the sails are in pretty bad shape. If you find these problems, take the sail to a local sailmaker for an evaluation.

Insurance

Just as with automobile loans, the lender of a marine mortgage will require proof of insurance coverage. Insurance costs can vary widely, depending on the class of boat and where it is being insured. Costs go up, for instance, in areas such as the southeast coast, where there are a lot of hurricanes and tropical storms. But rates differ from company to company as well. It is best to shop around before settling on any one insurance company, or you may end up paying a premium that is twice as high as it need be. You can expect at least a 1% deductible ($1,000 on a $100,000 boat). So, although insurance will pay for major repairs, it won't cover all the minor damages your boat will suffer in the course of a year.

The Marine Mortgage

The majority of us will have to seek financing when we buy a boat. In recent years, banks have become eager to lend money for boat purchases, although they sometimes can find the valuation of a boat difficult to determine.

The used boat market does not have the size and stability of the used car market or the consistent separation of wholesale from retail pricing. However, as is true of the automobile market, there are regularly published pricing reports. One of the most widely used is the BUC Used Boat Price Guide. Typically, it is dealers, brokers, banks, surveyors, and tax assessors who use the data. Using the pricing data in the BUC guides and in other pricing guides requires careful interpretation. Although for obvious practical reasons the data are not based on all boat sales, many years of collection and analysis have produced a reasonably reliable pricing guide, especially for boats in the larger sizes.

TIP

A must-have used boat guide is the BUC Used Boat Price Guide. Also known as the "blue book," it has a website at www.buc.com.

Once "market value" has been established, the lender and borrower can negotiate their down payment and interest rates as well as the appropriate collateral because the lender is confident that he knows how much the boat is worth.

The next obstacle is the establishment of clear title and non-encumbrances—liens, mortgages, etc. In most cases this is more difficult to determine in the boat market than in the automobile market. Brokers can be a big help with this.

Boat loans require a greater down payment on the borrower's part and often additional collateral in the form of a home mortgage. Typically, a marine mortgage carries with it the whole range of rights and obligations that accompany any property mortgage.

> After you own a boat you might want to join an organization such as **Boat/US** to take advantage of their discounts, towing service, insurance, and financing packages.

Actually owning a boat involves a lot more than just monthly loan payments. There are the overhead costs, like mooring or storage fees, insurance, and fuel. Depending on the type of mooring, the cost of moorage differs so much from area to area that it is impossible to estimate here what you might have to pay. Even in the same town, costs may range from as little as $6 a month per foot for a mooring to $30 a month for a slip in a popular marina. When you factor in electricity and water, the cost of a marina may be even higher. It is crucial that you investigate where you will keep your boat before you buy it so you can fit the cost within your budget.

You may discover that the marina you had planned on is far too expensive or that it has a waiting list of a few years. If you leave your boat on a mooring you will need to factor in the additional cost of using a launch to get to it. This can be another $50 to $250 per season. If, on the other hand, you decide to trailer your boat, you will need to buy a trailer and perhaps rent a storage facility to store it in, or store it in your yard. Again, prices will vary from region to region. Whatever your combination of storage and access is going to be, try to get a sense of what it will cost before you buy the boat. If you plan to buy a truck to haul your trailer around, factor in the cost of that, too.

Monthly repair costs for disposables, such as touch-up paint, varnishes, polishes, spare parts, etc., may run as high as $100. Then there's the cost of fuel. Oil and gas prices fluctuate, and this must be factored in. If you run out of fuel and the wind dies, you may need a tow back to harbor. The U.S. Coast Guard no longer provides towing. They will direct you to a commercial operator who may charge up to $300 for the tow if you are not a member of that operator's service.

Fitting Out

It's rare that a new boat comes with enough fenders, dock lines, ground tackle, and spare parts. You will need to buy these to outfit your boat. In addition you will have to purchase all the safety equipment you will need to commission the boat for insurance purposes, such as personal flotation devices, tool sets, fire extinguishers, first aid kits, flares, anchors, and anchor lines. Pick up a catalog from your local marine chandlery or hardware store and estimate prices accurately before you buy.

Since buying a used boat is legally complex, many buyers and sellers seek the help of a broker. When you're buying a used boat, it is crucial to find the right broker. While there are brokerage associations that endorse brokers, brokers tend to do business according to local custom. Their fees vary, and the range of service that they provide can vary a great deal, too.

Usually, a broker will make an agreement with a seller. Once the agreement is signed, the broker begins to advertise and show the boat. When the buyer and seller arrive at an agreeable price and terms, usually by working through the broker, then an agreement to purchase is drawn up based on a fairly standardized document.

An important aspect of this agreement to purchase is that a future closing date is specified. In the intervening time, the buyer can investigate title and search for state-registered bills of sale, chattel mortgages, and other claims, such as sales tax, that may exist on the boat.

Some brokers will agree to list a boat non-exclusively and will advertise it on a multiple-listing service. These services can be a great advantage to the buyer, to whom boats will be available not just locally, but nationally, and even worldwide using the Internet. If you have a broker who listens to your needs, you have a very good chance of finding just the right boat for you. It may be true that some brokers will try to push a boat you're not very interested in. But generally brokers who want to attract more business will do their best to accommodate you. If you are a first-time boat buyer, finding an experienced broker might be the wisest thing you can do.

BUYING A USED BOAT

M ost of us don't have enough knowledge to determine whether a boat is in good condition or not. We judge most boats on their appearance and appeal. This chapter offers tips on how to inspect a used boat, and how to use an expert to help you.

First Impressions: Trust Them

When you inspect a used boat for the first time, you quickly form an impression. A boat in good shape, looking smart, with a clean bilge, the woodwork nicely varnished or oiled, and the sails furled and trimmed nicely may have a premium price on it.

A boat that needs work might exhibit signs of mildew and mold on the deck, hull, and sails. Dirt and trash may have accumulated in corners and around drains, with rust running down the deck or hull from so-called stainless steel fittings. When you go inside the boat, you can smell bad plumbing or dirty bilges. Running your hands inside lockers and under shelves, you can feel moisture from leaks or condensation. This boat may seem like the bargain of the century, but unless you feel that it does not have structural problems and that you can restore it to its former glory, you should run, not walk, away from it.

We know that first impressions are not the whole story. A boat that looks, smells, and feels dirty could be a bargain if it only needs cleaning and a little work. Many people use "sweat equity" as a means of acquiring a boat that they don't have enough money to buy. That is, they are willing to put in the effort required to clean up a boat in ratty condition to get more boat for less money.

If you can't afford to pay the purchase price on a new boat or a big boat, your own labor could make up the difference. Remember that a boat that doesn't look great on first impression may be an excellent buy with some effort on your part. However, the unkempt boat may be a warning that it has never been maintained and that, under the surface, there are more problems. If you aren't interested in buying a boat that will require some work or repairs, keep on looking. If you like restoration and repair projects, try to assess your skills and available time. Can you complete a project of this size? If you need to, can you afford to hire someone to help you or finish the project for you? Answer these questions honestly before trying to restore or repair a used boat.

TIP

Don't let a bad trailer discourage you from buying a good boat.

A small boat, or one in which your investment is small, may not warrant the cost of a survey. Just the same, you need to examine your potential purchase very carefully to make sure there are no problems. If you ultimately expect to hire a surveyor, you can do some preliminary checking to narrow down the selection of boats. A quick look at a boat's appearance will indicate the care and maintenance a boat has received. If a boat is clean inside and out, it generally means that the owner took time to wash and scrub it on a regular basis. Mildew and grime accumulate when a boat has been ignored. On the following pages is a checklist of things to inspect. Some of the items listed do not apply to a dinghy or daysailer. However, this list will help you evaluate the whole range of sailboats, even those with complicated systems.

As you examine the boat closely, be prepared to discover items that don't necessarily meet your expectations. Maintain your objectivity as you make notes. If you find problems that you can't fix or ignore, then move on to another boat. Whether you want to buy a daysailer or an ocean cruiser, remember that there are many boats on the market. Examine several boats before you choose one.

TIP
Never use steel wool. It leaves rust marks.

Collect Your Tools

You'll need a few simple tools to inspect a boat. Take along a ruler, bronze wool, small mirror, flashlight, a rag or two, a magnifying glass, and a pencil and a notepad. The ruler will indicate if surfaces aren't flat. Bronze wool will wipe away rust so you can look for cracks. It takes a magnifying glass to see the hairline cracks in swaging. A small mirror is useful for looking behind hoses, engines, and other hard-to-see places. A flashlight is great for looking in the bilges and lockers. A rag keeps your hands clean if you get into grease and oil. You'll need a pencil and a notepad to keep your notes.

Armed with your tools and the checklist below, allow sufficient time to inspect the boat carefully. It is important to see a boat in and out of the water. If you have checked your in-the-water list and feel certain this is a boat you are interested in, then you will need to arrange to see it out of the water. If you think this is a potential purchase, you may want to wait until you've looked at several boats and then have the best one hauled out.

IN-THE-WATER CHECKLIST

This list should give you an idea of what to look for. Some solutions are proposed to give you an idea of the amount of work required to fix them.

Problem/Implication/Solution

1. **The boat lists (leans) to either side.** This does not affect the boat and can be corrected by moving weights around.

2. **The mast is not on the centerline.** It shouldn't take long to reset the mast on the centerline, unless the mast step is out of alignment. In this case the mast should be pulled out of the boat and the step realigned.

3. **The spreader angles are not the same port to starboard.** It will take five minutes in the bosun's chair to adjust them. Do not sail with the spreader angles out of whack. You could bring the rig down.

4. **There are popped strands on the rigging.** This is more serious. New rigging will be required.

5. **There are cracks or rust on the chain plates.** If the rust is superficial as it is on some types of cast stainless steel, don't worry about it. If it penetrates the surface, new chain plates may be required.

6. **The stanchions do not line up on both sides or are loose at the base and deck.** Generally, this means that the stanchions have been ground under a dock or bent coming alongside. Look for strain marks under the deck and crazing around the base of the stanchion. Also check to see if the area around the base of the stanchion is soft. Water may have penetrated the deck and may be rotting the deck core.

7. **The deck is uneven around the mast step.** The mast may have compressed the deck. Check under the deck to see if the deck is adequately supported.

8. **There are cracks in the fiberglass deck.** Cracks around the corners of the cabin house often show that the deck is not reinforced properly. Cracks around windows may mean that the window area is strained. (This often happens if a window is directly alongside the mast.) Star-shaped cracks elsewhere on the deck show that something heavy may have been dropped on it. Tap the deck lightly to see if it sounds mushy. If it does, the deck core may have to be replaced.

9. **The deck feels bouncy when you step on it.** On fiberglass boats decks can be bouncy without being weak. Trampolining, as it is called, is common on race boats that are built for lightness.

10. **Halyards and winches are hard to use.** You may have to relocate halyards and winches if your hands or arms hit lifelines or dodgers when using them. (Not a major job, but a pain just the same.)

11. **Sheaves on turning blocks, mainsheet, outhaul, and flattening and reefing gear don't rotate freely.** The solution is to remove them, clean the corrosion up and coat them with a little lanolin before reinstalling them. Often this problem is caused by corrosion between aluminum and the stainless steel.

12. **Tack, lifeline, gooseneck, and mainsheet shackle pins aren't held with cotters or rings.** Add cotter pins.

13. **Lifeline adjustments look loose.** Tighten them.

14. **Pelican hooks on lifelines aren't operational.** Replace them.

15. **Gate stanchions aren't braced.** Brace them.

Checking in the Cockpit:

16. **The view from the helm is obstructed.** This is a problem that, if you decide to buy the boat, you will have to make allowances for or fix. If the obstruction is a dodger post, the solution is to move your head. If it is something unmovable, look for another boat. This is a serious problem.

17. **The rudder and tiller are loose and sloppy.** Bearings are shot and need replacing.

18. **The wheel steering doesn't have stops.** An unusual problem, but one that can be fixed by putting bushings at the ends of the steering chain.

19. **The wheel brake isn't operational.** More examination will be needed to find out why.

20. **The engine gear and throttle levers are stiff.** The cable conduit needs greasing. This is a job that is done by forcing grease through the cable using a balloon-like device. Get the yard to do it. Another problem could be that the cable is turned around a corner too sharply. The solution is to ease the tight turn.

21. There are bubbles in the compass. Bubbles do no harm. They mean that the compass was left out in the sun. The alcohol expanded and vented out through the expansion port. The compass is still perfectly workable.

22. The compass lubber line is not straight. More of a problem: the compass will need to be replaced. Straighten the line and fill the compass with new alcohol. (Vodka will do in a pinch.)

Checking on the Foredeck:

23. Look for sturdy anchor-handling gear appropriate to the size and weight of the boat. That means that the anchors should be adequately sized, some chain fitted to the anchor line, and a nylon line shackled tightly to the chain. Ideally, the boat should have a chain stopper or devil's claw to hold the chain tightly when the anchor is down.

24. Make sure the bow is fitted with a proper size anchor roller and that the roller doesn't project too far over the bow, where it could be bent by the downward pull of the anchor line.

25. Make sure the anchor fits the roller and the anchor can be firmly pinned in place when the boat is underway.

26. Make sure the bitter end of the anchor rode is secured to a structural part of the vessel. A strong padeye in the anchor locker is the most usual method.

27. Operate the anchor windlass—both raising and lowering. With some of the modern low-profile windlasses you'll have to operate them from the helm station. Get a feel for how long the windlass will work before its overload switch cuts the power off.

28. Turn the roller-furling drum, if fitted, for synchronized, easy, even movement at top and bottom. Check to see if the roller-furler will work when under load.

Mast and Rig Inspection:

29. Standing at the side, sight up the mast for even pre-bend or straight line. Any sign of a bend means that you will have to retune the rig.

30. The drain holes in the mast base should be clear. While you are groping around down here, check for corrosion at the mast step.

31. Check for signs of mast corrosion and pitting, especially at the spreader ends and the sheave blocks.

32. Examine the swage terminations for cracking. You'll need a magnifying glass to look over the swages carefully. If you have any doubts, get them tested. If they are cracked your rig could fall down.

33. Make sure the turnbuckle pins are properly bent over and taped. Sharp cotter pins in rigging will tear sails, clothes, and skin.

34. Check if any strands are "popped" in wire rigging. If so, the rigging should be replaced.

Electrical System Check:

35. Make sure navigation lights operate and are visible to regulations. There should be spare anchor lights onboard, so check them, too.

36. Check that the steaming light operates.

37. Check that the anchor light operates.

38. Make sure the AC shore supply cord is not a trip hazard.

TIP

Beware of rewiring. Bad wiring can mean bad maintenance.

39. There should be a master AC breaker and a battery breaker switch. The automatic sump pump should operate when the battery is turned off.

40. The wiring should be to American Yacht and Boat Council (AYBC) specifications and marked properly.

41. There should be no wire terminations in the bilge. Any exposed terminals, switches, and light fixture contacts should be sprayed with CRC.

42. All instruments should be working properly. Check the Very High Frequency (VHF) radio by making a radio test. Check that the Global Positioning Satellite (GPS) antenna is not too high in the boat. If it is at the masthead, the GPS signal may be degraded.

What to Look for Below Deck

43. There are vents forward and aft providing adequate airflow.

44. The bunk size, number, and mattress thickness is acceptable.

45. The hatches and drawers latch. Ideally latches should not be a spring type that can rust.

46. The through hull valves open and close easily.

47. All hoses are double-clamped with stainless steel hose clamps.

48. Only USCG-approved fuel, heater, and stove hoses are used.

49. The water tanks have accessible valves and are vented. Fuel tanks should have all pipes going into and out of the top so that if a pipe springs a leak the fuel cannot drain into the bilge.

50. The installed manual bilge pumps work properly.

51. The stove is gimbaled.

52. The LPG switch is reachable from the appliance.

53. The chain plates are strongly bolted to the bulkheads.

54. The sole boards are firm and rest on strong bearers. You should be able to lift the sole boards easily, but they should be locked in place so that they wouldn't fly around the cabin if the boat were to capsize.

55. The bilges are clean and dry.

56. There is no sign of keel movement. Look at the hull/keel joint at the top of the keel. It will show a crack as the hull and keel expand at different rates, but you should not be able to get a fingernail into the gap.

Marine Toilet (Head)

57. The toilet rim should be above the float water line to prevent back flow. There should also be an anti-siphon valve on the intake line to prevent water being sucked into the head.

58. There should be a proper Y-valve for overboard discharge and the holding tank.

59. Anti-siphon loops should prevent return of discharge to the bowl.

Auxiliary Engine

60. The packing gland should be double-clamped and may drip. Water-lubricated glands drip a drop or two of water per hour.

61. Are there signs that any of the engine's containers for raw water, coolant, fuel, lubricant, or oil are leaky?

62. If there are signs of oil in the coolant, you've blown the block or have another major problem.

63. There are correct oil levels in the engine and transmission. Check the dipstick.

64. The alternator belt fits with a proper amount of play.

65. Engine compartment ventilation is adequate and blowers operate. (If the engine compartment is not ventilated properly the engine may be starved of air and will not run well.)

66. Engine-driven systems—freezer, pumps, watermaker, etc.—are working properly.

If you are satisfied that the in-the-water items present no major problems, then it is time to look at the boat out of the water.

The checklist below can be used for boats of all types, but it is primarily designed for fiberglass boats. Out of the water, look for these items:

1. Mismatched color indicating damage repaired. Most professionals will repaint the entire side rather than touch up, so mismatched color suggests that the repair may have been done by an amateur. Get a look at the inside of the repair to judge its quality.

2. Osmotic blisters can be a major problem. They generally happen to boats left in the water for more than a year. Seawater penetrates the gel coat and reacts with styrene in the hull laminate, causing a blister to pop up. If you spot osmotic blistering, move on—quickly. You do not want a boat where blisters are just developing. If the blistering has been fixed, the hull should be sound.

3. Crazing around bulkhead frame areas may indicate flexing of the frames where the mast load bears on them. If this shows up, you will have to get expert help to judge if it is critical.

4. A fracture in the rudder at the shaft entry is a major problem and should be fixed immediately. It is very difficult to sail home without a rudder.

5. Tap the rudder for signs of cavities or moisture. If the rudder drips for a week after the boat is hauled, you have water inside the blade. Your yard can advise you how to get it out.

6. Check if the rudder and the keel are in line. There isn't much you can do about it if they are not.

7. Make sure the rudder turns the same distance on both sides.

8. The propeller should be correctly placed on the shaft. There should be no more than one shaft diameter between the strut and the propeller.

9. Check the zincs to see if any electrolysis has taken place. If the zincs are missing, scrape the shaft, propeller, and all metal fittings for electrolysis. The bronze rudder will show up slightly pink. If you find a problem, get specialized help.

10. The keel-to-hull joint should be solid. It should show as a hairline crack around the top of the keel. A crack that you can fit a finger into means problems.

If you feel confident with your discoveries, discuss them with a boatyard to determine the cost of repairs. Then venture forward with a full survey.

Do You Need a Surveyor?

Buying a boat is exciting—maybe too exciting. It is easy to be so eager about the purchase of a boat that you forget to get it surveyed. Depending upon the size and age of the boat you want to buy, think about employing a marine surveyor whose profession is to evaluate boats. Getting your boat surveyed is like having a mechanic check on a used car that has caught your eye. Surveyors provide a professional opinion, unbiased by excitement. Simply put, the surveyor is there to help make sure that the boat is all it is advertised to be.

The notes you should have made while you were considering different boats will help to remind you of things you specifically want the surveyor to see. This will help save the surveyor's time. Go along when the boat is evaluated—and be prepared to ask questions.

Although you will receive a written report from the surveyor, be sure to take notes. The surveyor will probably take pictures during the course of the survey, but there is no reason that you can't take pictures, too, if it will help you to make up your mind.

Selecting the right surveyor

A good marine surveyor has a combination of skills that qualify him or her to evaluate boats for buyers, sellers, owners, insurance companies, and financial institutions. An experienced surveyor provides unbiased information about the value and structural condition of a boat.

Be forewarned that in most states marine surveyors are not licensed by any governmental body. There is no standard school curriculum for becoming a marine surveyor, although there are many correspondence and short-term programs available. The expertise of a surveyor comes from one thing: experience. An individual who has spent years sailing boats, working on boats, building boats, repairing boats, and using boats is someone who is likely to have accumulated the necessary experience and knowledge to be a marine surveyor.

Evaluating sailboats requires knowledge of hull construction, rigging, and systems. But surveyors tend to specialize, so you should look for someone whose specialty is yachts or pleasure boats. Within that group, you will want someone who specializes in the construction type of the boat you're considering. Wood, metal, and ferro-cement construction are particularly complex, and many surveyors are not familiar with the problems they present.

Before you start, ask the surveyor what the charge will be. If you need the job done to meet insurance and financing requirements, ask if he or she is on the recommended lists of the companies you want to use. You will need to know if the insurance company wants an "in-the-water" or an "out-of-the-water" survey. Later, you should get a complete written report. You have hired this person to represent your interests, so you want an individual who will do a thorough job. Since you are paying for the survey, the document created will be your private property. The surveyor may not give the information about your report to anyone else without your permission.

The survey will evaluate the equipment, age, and condition of the boat. There will be an analysis of the problems the surveyor discovers, with a list of ways to fix them. Some of the items may be simple, such as having fire extinguishers recharged; or they may be complex, such as osmotic blistering, which can be costly to repair. The surveyor will indicate market value, which may or may not reflect the need to complete the recommendations. For insurance purposes, the surveyor will also state the replacement value. A classic wooden yacht may have a low market value and a high replacement value, as the availability of skilled labor and materials is limited. Since the surveyor will not dismantle or open locked areas of a boat, there may be a disclaimer covering undetectable problems in inaccessible areas.

Most surveyors do not do an engine survey. They can make recommendations about taking engine oil samples for analysis and give you the names of people who will survey an engine. If you are buying a high-powered boat with expensive engines, get them looked at by a professional engine mechanic/surveyor.

There are three national organizations of **marine surveyors**:

The National Association of Marine Surveyors (NAMS) is the oldest. Applicants to NAMS must have been employed solely as surveyors for a period of years and must pass a written examination before they are admitted. Attendance at an annual conference is required to maintain membership status.

The Society of Accredited Marine Surveyors (SAMS) will accept new surveyors and provide some training courses.

Both organizations maintain geographic membership lists and toll-free numbers, so you can easily locate a surveyor in your area. Both also maintain websites: www.nams-cms.org or www.marinesurvey.org.

The Association of Marine Surveyors (ACMS) requires that surveyors have at least five years of work under their belts before registering with ACMS. The group has a certification program and holds annual programs and meetings. It's on the Web at www.acms-usa.com.

Surveys are valuable

When you buy a new boat, the bill of sale and commissioning information may satisfy the insurance and lending institutions. However, you will usually need a survey. New boats that are shipped a great distance, across country or across an ocean, may sustain damage in transit. In this case, the shipper or boat builder may pay for the survey.

Regulations and building practices vary from country to country. For a foreign-built boat, check with the dealer or get a surveyor to verify that it complies with U.S. regulations. When you take possession of your new boat, you may want a factory expert and an independent surveyor with you for a test sail. A surveyor's report will help you if warranty problems become an issue later.

When buying a used boat, you should have access to existing surveys. Ask the owner or broker if you can look at them. An old survey is not a substitute for your own report, but it is an indication of the boat's history. It may list equipment that is not onboard or recommendations that were never acted upon. It is one more tool to help you make a wise purchase.

CHAPTER 5

TRY BEFORE YOU BUY

W hether you are buying a used or a new boat, insist on a sea trial before completing the deal. This is not an unusual request. Any reasonable seller should agree to it. If you are buying a used boat, it's a good idea to bring a sailmaker or knowledgeable sailing friend along. Again, don't forget to take along your potential crew.

The Test Sail

If you're interested in a new boat, the actual boat you're going to buy might not be available for a trial. In fact, it may not even be built yet. In that case, the seller should take you out in an identical vessel. Your preliminary offer on the boat should include the stipulation that the performance of the two boats will be consistent. The good news is that if your boat isn't built yet, you may also be able to get things customized to suit needs or desires that show up during the test sail.

Put the boat through its paces

You wake up on the morning of your sea trial to a cloudless day with blue sky and no wind. A perfect day for sea trials? Not really. Sailboats need wind to go. This doesn't mean you should wait until gale-force winds are predicted, but you'll want the winds to be strong enough to make waves.

When you get to the dock, check to see whether the boat is floating level with the water. If it lists before anyone is in it, it will list even more when it's underway. Make sure that you're there when the engine is started for the first time that day. If the owner has warmed it up before you get there, you'll never find out if the engine has trouble starting. Check the temperature gauges to make sure they're cold before anyone flips the starting switch.

Before the boat leaves the dock, check that water is coming out of the exhaust. The exhaust smoke should have a slight tint, but not black or white. Back off the brake on the steering pedestal and check to see that the wheel moves easily.

Cruising and racing boats should have at least two bilge pumps, and you should check that both work. Ideally one will be accessible from the cockpit and the other run off the engine.

Under power (outboard)

Stand at the helm and check the visibility of engine gauges. Often they're under the seat and almost invisible. Check the location of any instruments. You should be able to read them from the helm easily. On most boats the engine controls are on the pedestal and easy to operate. If they are elsewhere, you will have to figure out how easy—or difficult—they are to operate.

On your way out of the harbor, see how the boat handles under power. Run the engine RPMs up as far as the dealer will let you and get a feel for whether the propellor is pushing the boat at a good speed or is laboring. If it is laboring, you may have to back off slightly on the pitch. Bring the boat to a stop and put it in idle. The boat should slip easily through the water. Now put the engine astern and see which way the prop kicks the stern. (RH props kick it to port.) Let it run astern for a moment and see if it is easy to get the boat to go where you want it to. If this task is difficult, you won't be able to back the boat into a slip. You'll have to drive it in frontways.

Put the engine in gear again and swing it around in a circle. See how small the radius of the circle is. If the circle is very wide, you may have problems turning into a tight marina or slip.

While you are running the engine, get a feel for the vibration. A lot of vibration may mean that a folding prop blade has not opened properly. Other types of vibration may indicate a misaligned engine. While someone else attends the engine, leave the helm and go below. Listen to the sound of the engine. If it is too loud to talk normally, it will need more sound-dampening insulation.

Now you're ready to hoist the sails.

Under sail

If you normally sit in the cockpit coaming or rail to steer, try sitting up there. Can you see the telltales on the headsail, or does your weight aft makes the boat drag its stern? If you race, you may have to get more crew weight forward to get the stern up out of the water.

Sit in the cockpit and see how comfortable it is. Ask your potential crew to check it out, too. If it is slightly uncomfortable, cushions will probably solve the problem. If the boat is really uncomfortable, you might want to make a different choice. This is a place where you'll be spending lots of time.

While you are on the helm, get a feel for the heel angle, the trim of the sails and the boat's weather (or lee) helm. If the helm feels heavy, it could be a problem with rudder balance, the size of the rudder, its sweepback, or just plain weather helm. If you think it is weather helm, try easing the mainsheet down on the traveler to see if the helm lightens up.

Take a look up the mast to make sure that it is still straight, both fore and aft and transversely. If the mast is standing straight up, look to see how much weather helm the boat has. It should have almost nothing if the wind is under ten knots. As the wind increases, expect weather helm to increase. When the wind is blowing about 15 to 20 knots you will have to reef. In general, assume that boats with a fairly flat bottom (light displacement, good performance) will reef earlier than heavier boats with more deeply veed hulls.

Check to see how easy it is to move the mainsail under load. If the mainsheet is impossible to move when the boat is beating to windward, you may want to specify a larger winch or a different mainsheet system.

Make a few tacks and see how easy it is to get the headsail through the fore triangle. If the boat has a midstay, it might be quite difficult to tack it and you may have to partially roller furl the jib in order to tack. If the boat is a cruiser, you may find that tacking is simply a matter of putting the helm over so that the club-footed headsail flops over on the other tack along with the mainsail. No muss, no fuss.

Check to see that you can read the instruments when you need to. Remember that the electronic instruments follow the antics of the boat, so they are always lagging behind the steering. Nevertheless, the depth sounder should be clearly visible, as should the compass, which should have a dimmer switch for nighttime use.

▲ Remember to bring your crew along with you for any test sail.

Movement on deck

While you are moving around on deck and checking everything, notice the handholds. Are they in the right place? See how easy it is to get forward or aft on deck and whether you feel comfortable. See if you can operate the halyards, winches, and lines on your own. You may need to hold onto the boat with one hand and work with the other.

Winches

First look at the winches to see if the drums are scored. (If a wire halyard is used on an alloy drum it can get quite badly scored.) You can probably get new drums for Lewmar winches, but older Barients and Barlows are no longer made and you will have to replace the winch. Next, make sure each winch revolves properly under load and that the handle turns easily when under a full strain. Often winches installed by the manufacturer of a new boat are marginally sized and are working at the top of their range. You might need to go one size larger later. Finally, check to see that there are enough winch handles.

Sheets and guys

If the sheets are stiff, it often means that they haven't been washed in years. Salt accumulates in braided sheets and causes them to stiffen. Soak each sheet in a bucket of warm water for a few hours, then rinse it thoroughly in fresh water to get rid of salt. Check for wear on all the sheets and look for herniated casings. Make sure that any shackles (on spinnaker guys) are not bent and that they open easily.

Mainsail controls

First, take a look at the mainsheet system. Check to see that it is easy to operate under load, that you can move the traveler when the main is tightly sheeted, and that all controls operate easily. Now sit in your normal helming position and make sure you can reach the traveler and the mainsheet. On smaller boats in a gusty northerly wind you might have to steer and play the mainsail. Check that you can reach the backstay adjuster (on boats to 25 feet LOA), that you can operate the main (getting it in and out), that you can hold the tiller, that you can see the jib tell-tales, and that you can balance yourself on the high side.

On larger boats make sure that you and your crew can operate all of the gear listed at right. Your crew should also be able to adjust the main cunningham, vang, and outhaul while the boat is sailing to windward. While this is not so important on a cruising boat, it is highly important on a race boat, especially if the crew must keep their weight to windward.

On used boats check to see that all mainsail controls can be led to operable winches if necessary, that all the inside-the-boom gear is in good shape, and that the boom is high enough not to crack people on the head as the boat is tacked or jibed.

If the boat is fitted with a hydraulic vang, make sure it can support the boom as well as pull it down. If it supports the boom, there is no need for a topping lift, which may chafe the mainsail leech. Once you own the boat, sew tell-tales to the batten pockets of the mainsail to help you trim it properly.

Look at the reefing gear. Ideally, each reef should remove about 20% of the sail. If the reef points show signs of strain, the mainsail cloth should be looked over carefully. Check to see that the reef cringles at each end of the reef are not distorted. If they are, this tells you that the mainsail has been stressed. Try putting in a reef to see how easy it is. If you cruise, you may have to put the reef in on your own.

Headsail controls

The headsail is controlled by the roller furling gear on cruising boats and by several other controls on race boats. When using roller furling gear, check to see if the sail can be rolled up under load. Often it cannot, which means that you must let the headsail sheet go before you can furl the sail. Check the headstay sag on the roller furling gear. Often a roller furler headstay sags more than a non-roller furler. You should adjust the rig to eliminate as much sag as possible. Eliminating sag will help keep the boat upright and sail faster. As the sail is rolled up when the breeze increases, the top and bottom of the stay tend to rotate more than the middle of the stay. Consequently, the sail gets baggier. Having a sagging headstay and a baggy sail heels the boat even more, requiring you to roll in more headsail to keep the boat on its feet.

If you plan to race the boat, check to see that the Cunningham line is easy to operate, that the sail track cars move easily under load, that the headsail sheeting angles are suitable for the type of headsail you will use, and that the leads from the sail clew to the winches are clean and will not snag.

RUNNING RIGGING

While standing rigging supports the mast, running rigging is used to raise and trim sails. Check to make sure winches are adequately sized and operate properly. Check, too, that the traveler and track cars move easily. While most of the problems that surface are minor and easily correctable, replacing all the halyards and one or two winches can add up to a substantial investment.

Running rigging may include:

- Halyards to hoist the sails aloft. They are nowadays almost always run inside the mast to reduce windage.
- Topping lifts to hoist booms or spinnaker poles to the desired height.
- Headsail sheets to control the headsail.
- The mainsheet to control the tension in the leech of the mainsail.
- The mainsheet taglines, usually made of Dacron, are used to control the angle of the mainsail to the wind.
- The outhaul to adjust the foot of the mainsail.
- The Cunningham line to tighten the luff of the sail and pull the draft forward. (A Cunningham can be both on the main and on the jib and is used mostly on racing boats.)
- Reefing lines to reduce sail area when reefing (rolling the sail from its foot).
- Downhauls, which are not often seen but are used to pull down on any sail.
- A preventer to keep a boom from swinging across the boat in a violent jibe when the boat is sailing downwind.
- Spinnaker sheets and guys to control the foot of the spinnaker.

To avoid confusion in the cockpit, it helps to color-code all the lines. For example, the jib halyard can be red, with jib sheets red-and-white striped. The mainsail halyard can be blue, with the mainsheet blue and white. The traveler taglines can be blue and green, as can the vang, while the Cunningham is blue and white.

Movement below deck

Go below and get a feel for how easy it is to navigate the companionway when the boat is heeled. Reach for handholds and see if they are where they should be. Check to see if you can use the head in a seaway. Often, any water in the head will slop out as the boat bounces over waves, so you might have to turn off the seacock when at sea. This is OK for short trips, but not if you plan on a three- or four-day cruise that includes sailing overnight.

While you are below deck, check the front and back edges of windows for leaks, which generally show up as brown streaks on the trim. Look for traces of leaks in the overhead. Also look at the overhead to see if it has been removed a lot. If it has, you can suspect that the boat has had electrical problems in the past. Ask the owner about this.

TIP
You might want to rent a few different boats to see how they handle before you buy. It can be well worth the rental fees.

Check all the ship systems to see how well they function at sea. Turn on the radar when the boat is heeled. Can you see the ocean only on the lee side? If so, you may have to gimbal the radar antenna. Check to see if the nav lights, the overhead lights, and the bilge pumps work when the boat is heeled.

Now for the most important thing: how do you and your crew like being aboard? Are you comfortable? Do you feel that the boat is for you? Do you feel safe aboard? Is the stowage sufficient? Is the galley workable both when the boat is upright and when it is heeled? Are the toilet and shower facilities adequate? Is everyone looking forward to spending long periods of time onboard?

Only by making all these checks and getting a good feel for the boat on a sea trial can you find out if this is the boat for you. There is a lot of work to do in a short time, and you will have to get the seller to give you enough time to get it all done. If you don't get a feel for the boat while it is underway, you may find things that you do not like after you own the boat. That's not what you want to do. What you do want is to look forward to every cruise or race without being worried about what works and what doesn't.

Chartering as a trial

If you're interested in a new boat, the actual boat you're going to buy might not be available for a trial. In that case, the dealer or seller may offer an identical vessel for the day. Your preliminary offer on the boat should include the stipulation that the performance of the two boats will be consistent. However, boat builders offer many different engine options. The boat you try may have a different engine from the one you buy and this will affect performance and handling.

If you cannot get a boat for a sea trial, the alternative is to charter an identical boat for the day. Charter operators will not let a novice climb into a boat and take off. If you don't have enough experience yourself, you might hire someone to operate the boat, or you could bring an experienced friend or family member along. Either way, once the boat is underway you should be able to take the wheel for a while in open water. You can learn a lot about how a boat handles in just a short period of time.

If you want to get a feel for a boat's capabilities as a cruiser, you could also arrange for an on-dock or on-the-water weekend charter. Spending a weekend tied up at a dock might not sound exciting. But it will give you an idea of what it might be like to be aboard with another adult and perhaps a couple of kids for any length of time on the boat that you are about to buy. If you can meander around your favorite cruising grounds for a weekend, you will know exactly how your new boat will fit into the family cruising experience.

PART II

OUTFITTING

After you have purchased your boat, you will probably need to fit it out. First, you should make sure you have all the safety features required by law, then you should add some useful gear, such as fenders, anchors, and lines. Only after you have the essentials onboard should you think about gear to enhance your boating experience.

CHAPTER 6

STAYING SAFE

A ccording to the U.S. Coast Guard (USCG), several hundred lives could be saved each year if every boater were to wear a life jacket. Although your safety depends on the type of boat you use and the nature of the sailing that you do, the regulations on USCG-approved safety equipment are mandatory for all boats. It is your legal responsibility to carry the required equipment listed on pages 88 to 93, to keep that equipment in proper working order, and to operate your boat in a safe manner.

PERSONAL FLOTATION DEVICES

Any time anyone goes sailing, they are at risk of falling overboard or of the vessel sinking. A personal flotation device (PFD), otherwise known as a life jacket, is designed to keep your head above water and assist you in maintaining a position that permits proper breathing.

Everyone aboard the boat needs a PFD. Children should wear PFDs at all times. In some states, the law states that all children six and under must wear them while onboard; in other states, it is all children under twelve. Adult non-swimmers, anyone boating alone, anyone wearing a cast, or anyone who must do a job that could result in being swept overboard must wear a PFD whenever the boat is underway.

The USCG classifies PFDs into five types. (In Europe, Safety of Life at Sea- (SOLAS-) approved life jackets that offer up to 35 pounds of buoyancy are the norm.) The USCG-approved categories are:

► Type I

A Type I PFD is the easiest to pull on in an emergency. It provides the most buoyancy and is effective for all waters, especially open, rough, or remote waters requiring extended survival. It is designed to turn most unconscious wearers to a face-up position. Type I is available in jacket or bib models, as shown. The adult size provides at least 22 pounds of buoyancy, the child size, 11 pounds minimum.

► Type II

The Type II "horse-collar" or near-shore buoyant vest is intended for calm, inland water or wherever there is a good chance of quick rescue. The turning action is not as pronounced or as effective for as many people as Type I. An adult size provides at least 15 1/2 pounds of buoyancy; a medium child size provides 11 pounds. Infant and small child sizes each provide at least 7 pounds of buoyancy.

► Type III

The Type III is generally the most comfortable and popular type of PFD. It's made of foam, rather than the more bulky kapok, and is available in many styles, colors, and sizes. Also known as a flotation aid, a Type III PFD is good for calm, inland water, or where there is a good chance of a quick rescue. It has the same minimum buoyancy as Type II. However, the wearer may have to tilt his or her head back to avoid turning face down in the water.

► Type IV

The Type IV is a throwable device designed for calm inland water with heavy boat traffic, where help is always present. It is not designed to be worn, but rather to be thrown to a person in the water, then grasped and held by the user until the rescue occurs. Type IV devices include horseshoe buoys (approved for use in the U.S.), ring buoys, and buoyant cushions.

► Type V

The Type V is the least bulky of all PFD types. It contains a small amount of inherent buoyancy and an inflatable chamber. When it is inflated, its performance is equal to a Type I, II, or III PFD. USCG regulations also recognize certain Type V special-purpose devices, including wet suits, deck suits, and whitewater types.

► Inflatable lifejackets

Inflatable life jackets are officially classified as Type VI and have become extremely popular. They fit like a normal collar with the vest folded inside the collar. If the wearer goes over the side, the jacket can either be manually inflated or inflate automatically. Manually-inflated jackets operate with a simple tug on a lanyard. This sets off the compressed air cylinder and the life jacket fills. The wearer needs to be conscious to operate the lanyard. Auto-inflating jackets operate as soon as the igniter tablet gets wet.

INVENTORY OF COMMONLY USED

In addition to PFDs and fire extinguishers (see page 95), flame arresters, sound signaling devices, and visual distress signals are also legally required by the USCG. Here is a list of other useful equipment.

*Indicates items required by the U.S. Coast Guard

Bilge pump or bailer

Although federal regulations do not require dewatering devices—a bucket or other bailer on unpowered boats or electric bilge pumps on boats with engines—they are required by some state laws. Required or not, these items are recommended for safe boating. The Ocean Racing Council (ORC) recommends that boats have at least two bilge pumps, one of which is operable from the cockpit. Most manufacturers use the ORC recommendations as a basic standard.

Boathook

A hook on a pole is invaluable for fending off, placing lines over pilings, picking up pennants of mooring buoys, and recovering articles dropped over the side. When marked with rings at one-foot intervals—a mark in a different color or size should be added for the boat's draft—a boathook is useful for probing around a stranded boat in search of deeper water.

Charts and navigation publications

Essential for planning your course and navigating safely, charts and navigation publications, such as those covered in Chapter 9, should be up-to-date. For trip planning, you can use an electronic chart on your computer. These charts are as extensive as, and in some cases, more extensive than, paper charts. Their cost is around $100 to $250 depending on the manufacturer.

Compass

Desirable on any boat for both emergency and regular use, a compass and plotting instruments are recommended for piloting purposes.

Detectors and alarms

A well-thought-out alarm system can alert you to a wide variety of dangers, from burglars on deck to explosive vapors trapped below.

A float switch mounted above the normal bilge-water level can signal flooding in the bilge and turn on the bilge pump. Other detectors indicate

angerous levels of gasoline, propane, hydrogen fumes, or carbon monox-
le. Additional sensors can warn of low oil pressure, loss of engine coolant,
nd fire. For detecting burglars coming aboard, neither home nor automo-
ile alarms are practical aboard an occupied boat; only install an alarm that
specifically designed for marine use.

Very High Frequency (VHF) Radio

ne VHF radio is the most basic piece of electronic safety equipment
sed onboard boats. It can be used to receive weather reports,
essages, and Coast Guard warnings. It can also be used to call for
ssistance. See Chapter 9 for a description of other electronic
quipment that you may want to have aboard.

Emergency Position-Indicating Radio Beacon (EPIRB)

is automatic radio transmitter, described in Chapter 9, should be
rried on any boat operating offshore.

Fenders

rried in appropriate sizes and numbers, fenders are used for normal berthing,
d when one boat must make fast to another while underway or at anchor.

First-aid kit

n essential item of safety equipment, the kit (see Chapter 10), should be
companied by a first-aid manual and supplemented by one or more first-aid
urses.

Flame arrester*

ith some minor and technical exceptions, every inboard gasoline engine must
e equipped with an acceptable means of backfire flame control—or "flame
rester." Flame arresters no longer require USCG approval; the USCG now
cepts flame arresters complying with Underwriters Laboratories (UL)
andard 1111 or Society of Automotive Engineers (SAE) J1928. When in use,
me arresters must be secured to the air intake of the carburetor with an air-
ght connection. Elements must be clean, and grids must be tight enough
prevent flames passing through. Note that many engines are now using
ectronic Fuel Injection (EFI), which eliminates the need for a flame arrester.

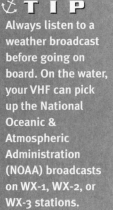

⚓ T I P

Always listen to a weather broadcast before going on board. On the water, your VHF can pick up the National Oceanic & Atmospheric Administration (NOAA) broadcasts on WX-1, WX-2, or WX-3 stations.

Flashlight or searchlight

A searchlight—installed on larger craft, hand-held on smaller boats—serves both as a night piloting aid and as an emergency signaling device. A multi-cell flashlight or electric lantern can serve these functions, although sometimes less effectively.

Ground tackle

Ground tackle includes anchors, anchor rode (line or chain), and all the shackles and other anchoring gear. All ground tackle must be in operational condition. After use, it should be carefully re-stowed so that the main anchor is ready for use and auxiliary and storm anchors are readily accessible.

Leadline

A hand-held leadline is useful as a backup to the electronic depth sounder. A dollop of wax or hard grease is affixed to the bottom of the lead to obtain a sample of bottom material, which will help you choose the right anchor.

Life rafts

Standards for life rafts—size, capacity ratings, seaworthiness, sturdiness—are set by SOLAS international conventions, and are adapted for the U.S. by the USCG. For everyone who sails offshore, a SOLAS-approved inflatable life raft should be considered mandatory. For racing boats, ORC regulations insist on SOLAS-approved life jackets.

Lightning protection

Lightning strikes a number of boats every year, especially in Florida and other southern states. Lightning protection aboard your boat could help avoid considerable damage to your boat and may save the lives of those aboard. Two types of lightning protection should be installed—one to guide the charge of a main strike safely down into the water, the other to protect electronic equipment from a damaging power surge.

In recent years the thinking about boats and lightning strikes has changed. It is now believed that a bottle-brush style ion-dissipator helps to disperse the ions that cause lightning in the first place. Dissipator manufacturers claim that boats using a dissipator have never been struck by lightning.

Sound signaling devices*

The *Navigation Rules* require sound signals to be made under certain circumstances, including meeting, crossing, and overtaking other boats. (These situations are described in the *Rules*.) All vessels, including recreational vessels, are required to sound fog signals during periods of reduced visibility. So, you must have some means of making an efficient sound signal. Vessels 39.4 feet or more in length are required to carry on board a whistle (or horn) for marine use and a bell. In an emergency, you can use any loud noise to attract attention. Use a loud hailer, or make a megaphone from a rolled up chart, or bang on a metal pot.

Spare parts and tools

The list of tools and spare parts to be carried on board is best developed by skippers for their own boats. It will vary, depending on the type of boat, how it is normally used, and the capabilities of the crew. The list may include items for making emergency repairs at sea, such as simple tools, plugs, cloth, screws, nails, wire, and tape. Spare bulbs for the navigation lights, and various mechanical and electrical spare parts may also be included.

Visual distress signals*

Most boats—and all boats operating offshore and on the Great Lakes—must be equipped with visual distress signals, classified by the USCG for day use only (D), night use only (N), or combined day-and-night use (D/N). If pyrotechnic signals are used, the minimum quantity is three each of D and N signals, or three D/N signals. Each device must be readily accessible and certified as com- plying with USCG requirements. Replace distress and smoke flares, as well as meteor rockets, after 42 months from the date of manufacture.

USCG regulations prohibit any display of visual distress signals except when assistance is required. Use emergency signals only when in distress, and only when help is close enough to see the signal.

ACR Electronics makes a special light called the SOSearchlight. It flashes an SOS signal that is visible for over 18 miles at night. Rather than send up a flare and hope someone sees it, the SOS light can run for hours on one battery. It is approved by the USCG.

On sailboats, lifelines serve as boundaries for the deck, particularly when children or pets are aboard. Many people reinforce those boundaries by rigging nylon netting along the lifelines, or between the hulls of multihulls. Small children are adventurous, however, and the boat can pitch, roll, or heel; safety harnesses provide additional safety insurance.

Harnesses are also essential in other conditions for boaters of all ages. They will keep you aboard even if you fall, and should be worn anytime you are sailing alone, whenever any crew member is on deck in heavy weather, when going on deck alone at night while underway, when going aloft, or whenever you feel there is a danger that you might lose your footing.

Each safety harness aboard your boat should be adjusted to fit the person who will wear it, then labeled to ensure quick identification when needed in an emergency. Stow your harnesses in dry places and inspect them regularly for wear and tear.

Harnesses should be clipped to jacklines that run along the deck. When installing jacklines, make sure that they end at least six feet ahead of the transom. That way, if you fall off and are clipped to the jackline, you can still reach the boat's transom to pull yourself back aboard.

Fueling

Before starting out make sure you have enough fuel on board, and if any is needed, fill the tank safely. When you fuel your boat with diesel, before filling, wipe the deck down with a soapy sponge. That way if you spill fuel it will be easy to clean up. If you take on fuel in a foreign port, filter it through a funnel as it goes into your tank to keep sediment from getting into the tank. If you fill a gas engine, make sure that anything that can create a spark, such as cigarettes, electric motors, and galley pilot lights, is turned off and that a fire extinguisher is close by.

TIP

When fueling your boat, wipe the area around the fuel fill with a soapy sponge before you undo the fill. That way if any fuel spills, the soapy area will prevent it from soaking into or staining the deck.

Fire extinguishers

On board a boat, fire extinguishers are required if any one or more of the following conditions exist:

▶ There are inboard or inboard/outboard engines on the boat.

▶ There are closed compartments where fuel tanks are stored.

▶ There are closed stowage compartments in which flammable or combustible materials are stored.

▶ There are double bottoms that are not sealed to the hull or are not completely filled with flotation materials.

▶ There are closed living spaces.

▶ The boat has permanently installed fuel tanks.

Approved extinguishers are classified by a letter and number symbol. Type B, commonly used on boats, is designed to put out fires involving flammable liquids such as gasoline, oil, and grease. BI and BII extinguishers both contain foam, CO_2, dry chemicals, or non-flammable gas. Just like PFDs, extinguishers should be easily accessible.

FIRE EXTINGUISHER CONTENTS				
Class	Foam in gals.	CO_2 in lbs.	Dry Chemical in lbs.	Halon in lbs.
B-I	1.25	4	2	2.5
B-II	2.50	15	10	10.0

Boat registration

Sailboats must be registered in the state of primary use. You can get the numbers and license at the state tax collector's office. A boat number begins with a two-letter state designation, followed by not more than four digits and not more than two letters. Between the letter and number groups there must be a hyphen or space. Numbers should be displayed in bold block letters on both sides of the boat's forward half. States usually require that a validation sticker be displayed, confirming that registration fees have been paid.

TIP

Don't drink and drive! Boating while intoxicated (BWI) is against the law, just like DWI. So save that bottle of Dom Perignon for dry land. On the water, keep your head clear.

The average set of sails is designed for moderate wind, not for heavy weather. As wind strength increases, the first step is to put in a reef or change to a smaller headsail. If you have a lot of weather helm, you put in a reef first. If you have none, or lee helm, make the headsail smaller first.

Reefing is done primarily to keep the boat upright as the wind increases. To reef you can roll the sail around the boom as some of the latest reefing systems do, you can roll it into the mast as some mast-rolling systems do, or you can put in a reef. There are several types of reefs. Jiffy reefing uses a single line led through the mainsail reef clew and then forward around the mainsail reef tack point and to a winch. When the halyard is eased, the entire reef is put in by hauling on the reefing line. Slab reefing, recommended for cruisers, uses a line at the reefing clew of the sail and another at the reefing tack. When the halyard is eased, both lines are tensioned and the sail is reefed. On racing boats the tack line is dispensed with and the reef cringle is pulled down and snapped over a tack horn on the front of the boom. This quick method is often used by single-handed sailors.

When the reef is installed it should be tied in—that is, reef lines from each reef point should be tied around the boom. This distributes the load on the foot of the sail along the entire boom rather than leaving it on the reefing cringles. Most boats have three sets of reefs. After the third set of reefs has been installed, if the wind continues to build, the skipper must resort to using the storm trysail. The storm trysail is a really small sail that fits into the luff groove and is sheeted to the deck. The mainsail boom is lowered and lashed down on deck to prevent it from waving around in heavy wind and seas.

At the front of the boat, cruisers roll up their headsail as the wind increases. This has the effect of making the sail slightly baggier and contributes to increased heel angle. (Some sailmakers add a foam luff to their roller furling sails to help reduce the bagginess.) As the wind increases, the roller-furled sail is rolled away until it, too, disappears. If the wind is so strong that the sail must be rolled up, wrap a few turns of the sheet around the sail to prevent it from unrolling. At this point, the prudent sailor should set a storm jib. Talk to your sailmaker if you wish to fit a storm jib.

Safety On Board

From the moment you begin to plan your boating excursion to the moment you return, there are steps you can take to ensure that everyone aboard has a safe trip. Planning starts with a "float plan" written before you even leave the house. It tells someone where you are going and when you plan to return, so someone who is not onboard will know to start worrying if you don't arrive home on time. Leave the plan with a responsible friend or family member. Just remember to check back in as soon as you're back on land or if you change your itinerary.

PRE-DEPARTURE FLOAT PLAN

1. **NAME AND PHONE NUMBER OF PERSON REPORTING**

2. **DESCRIPTION OF BOAT** Type of boat; color of hull, deck and cabin; trim; registration number; length; name of boat; make; any other distinguishing features.

3. **PERSONS ABOARD** Name, age, address, telephone number of skipper and each crew member.

4. **MEDICAL PROBLEMS OF ANY PERSON ABOARD**

5. **ENGINE TYPE** Horsepower, number of engines, fuel capacity.

6. **SAFETY AND SURVIVAL EQUIPMENT** Personal flotation devices, flares, mirror, visual distress signals, flashlight, food, paddles, water supply, anchor, life raft, dingy, EPIRB, and any other safety or emergency equipment you may have aboard.

7. **MARINE RADIO** Type, frequencies.

8. **TRIP EXPECTATIONS** Departure points, route, destination, expected date and time of arrival. Expected date of return.

9. **VEHICLE LICENSES** Color, make and license number of automobile and trailer (if applicable), and where they are parked.

10. **SUGGESTED DATE AND TIME TO CALL COAST GUARD OR LOCAL AUTHORITY FOR SEARCH**

11. **TELEPHONE NUMBERS TO CALL FOR FURTHER INFORMATION OR IN CASE OF EMERGENCY**

12. **COMPETENCY OF PEOPLE ABOARD** Boating skills and emergency first-aid training.

BOATING SAFETY CHECKLIST

I s your boat as safe as it can possibly be? If you can answer "Yes" to the following questions, chances are that the vessel is safely equipped and that you operate it safely.

- ► Do you carry legally required and other safety equipment aboard? Do you know how to use it?

- ► Before getting underway and with everyone aboard, do you review emergency procedures and identify all safety equipment and exits (where appropriate)?

- ► If you carry a life raft aboard your boat, have you included the proper deployment as part of your routine safety training? At least one other crew member should know, for example, where the raft is located, how to inflate it quickly and to inflate it on deck rather than below decks or in the cockpit.

- ► Are you aware that it is illegal to operate a vessel while intoxicated? Most states use .08 ppm as the minimum blood alcohol level for recreational boaters. However, the USCG still has to make the arrest. When alcohol or drugs are mixed with boating, the results can be fatal. A large percentage of all boating accidents are alcohol-related.

- ► Do you check local weather reports before departure, and keep the VHF NOAA weather radio on, as well as keep a weather eye open during your sail? Do you know what different types of clouds mean?

- ► Are your lifesaving equipment and fire extinguishers readily accessible at all times?

- ► Do you avoid overloading your boat with people or gear?

- ► Do you make sure you have good non-skid surfaces on deck and on the soles of shoes of everyone aboard?

- ► Do you keep bilges clean and electrical contacts tight?

- ► Do you guard rigidly against any fuel system leakage?

- ► Have you requested a Coast Guard Auxiliary Courtesy Marine Examination for the current year?

- Have you taken any safe boating courses or first-aid courses?
- Before departing, do you leave a float plan so someone knows where you are boating and when you are expected to return? Do you notify the holder if plans change?
- Are you familiar with the waters that you will be cruising, so you can deal with tides, currents, sandbars, and any other hazards you may encounter?
- Do you know your personal limitations and responsibilities? Remember that exposure to sun, wind, and cold water affect your ability to react.
- Are you aware that a sailboat mast touching a power line could electrocute you? Check your clearances while underway.
- If you are a non-swimmer, are you planning to learn to swim? It could save your life or someone else's.
- Are you and your crew prepared for any emergencies that could occur?
- Do you watch and heed posted speeds? Do you slow down in anchorages?
- When anchoring, do you allow adequate scope? Are you far enough away from neighboring boats?
- If someone falls into the water, do you know what to do? Avoid jumping in; use a reaching, throwing, or floating assist such as a paddle, a cushion, a Type IV PFD life ring, or a rescue line with a float attached.
- Do you avoid relieving yourself over the side of the boat in a standing position? This is a common cause of falling off the boat.
- Do you know that standing in a small boat raises the center of gravity, often to the point of capsizing? Standing for any reason or even changing position in a small boat can be dangerous, as is sitting on the gunwales or seat backs or in a pedestal seat while underway.

TEN STEPS TO SAFETY MAINTENANCE

Most marine safety equipment needs some sort of maintenance—ranging from regular, ongoing attention to periodic checks at weekly, monthly, or annual intervals. Following the guidelines below, custom-design a checklist for your particular boat, adding to it as you install or modify equipment. Make an entry in the boat's log of all inspections, tests, and servicing of fire extinguishers. Not only will this record essential checks; it may prove valuable for insurance surveys or claims. Remember, follow-up repair is just as important as periodic checks. Never delay maintenance related to safety, and avoid operating a boat that has any safety defect.

1. Keep your bilge absolutely free of dirt and trash. Check frequently and clean it out as often as needed. Accumulations of dirt, sawdust, wood chips, and trash in the bilge will soak up oil and fuel drippings. In addition to creating a fire hazard, this may also clog limber holes—drainage holes—and bilge pumps.

2. Inspect lifesaving equipment. At the beginning and midpoint of each boating season, check the condition of all lifesaving equipment (see pages 88 to 93). Replace inadequate lifesaving devices immediately. Attempt repairs only where full effectiveness can be restored; if in doubt, ask for USCG advice.

3. Test fire extinguishers periodically by discharging them. In addition to good maintenance, this provides valuable practice. Discharge one of the portable units each year on a regular rotation basis—preferably in the form of a drill with all crew members participating. Away from the boat, put out an actual small fire in a metal pan or tub. When discharging a CO_2 extinguisher, always hold the nozzle by the plastic handle; never unscrew the hose from the cylinder to discharge it openly. Always discharge a dry-chemical extinguisher completely.

After an extinguisher has been removed for testing or practice discharge, have it serviced by a competent shop and reinstalled as soon as possible. Make sure that there are always enough extinguishers aboard to serve your boat's safety needs.

4. Check the engine and fuel system frequently for cleanliness and leaks. If you find any leaks, take immediate action. Wipe up any oil or grease drippings and stop leaks as soon as possible. Do not use the boat, and—with all loads turned off so that no sparks will jump—disconnect the leads from the battery so the engine cannot be started.

5. Check the entire fuel system annually, inch by inch, including fuel lines in areas not normally visible. When replacing fuel system components, use equivalent replacement parts, never automotive parts. If any joints or lengths of tubing or hose are worn or damaged, call a qualified mechanic without delay.

6. Have a qualified professional inspect your boat's electrical system thoroughly every year, including all wiring in areas not normally visible.

Search for any cut or chafed insulation, corrosion at connections, excessive sag or strain on conductors, and other visible signs of deterioration. Test leakage by opening each circuit at the main distribution panel with all loads turned off to measure current flow. Ideally, there should be no current flow; current of more than a few milliamperes indicates electrical leakage that should be identified and corrected without delay.

Keep in mind that connections at the boat's storage batteries need special attention. Disconnect them and use a wire brush to remove all corrosion. Next, replace and tighten the connections, then apply a light coat of grease or other protective substance.

7. Maintain your boat's bilge ventilation system in top operating condition.

8. Check underwater fittings annually. This includes shafts, propellers, rudders, struts, stuffing boxes, and metal skegs. Repack stuffing boxes as often as necessary to keep them from leaking excessively, while also checking shafting for alignment and excessive wear at strut bearings. Examine propellers to see if they need truing up.

9. Choose replacement parts carefully. Whatever parts you replace—for fuel, electrical, or ventilation systems; navigation light bulbs; or anything aboard your boat—make sure you use equivalent components that are designed specifically for marine use.

10. Perform an annual safety inspection of the hull and fittings below the waterline. On wooden boats, check hull planking for physical damage and for any general deterioration from age. Check fiberglass hulls for any cracks, especially at points of high stress. Call in an expert if you find any suspicious areas.

You should **test all PFDs** periodically to make sure they have retained their buoyancy. The most instructive way of doing this is by putting one on and jumping into a pool or shallow water. Not only will this test each life jacket, but it will give you some experience of getting into and using one. This is especially important for inflatable jackets. (It is very hard to read the instructions after you have fallen off the boat.) After every use, wash the life jacket with fresh water. Always air-dry your PFDs thoroughly. Store them in a dry, well-ventilated, easily accessible place on the boat during summer and off the boat during the long months of winter storage.

Seasickness

Seasickness is important to know about and understand. If you get seasick, your trips may be no fun at all. If you get severely sick whenever you go on a boat, you may be best off moving inland and taking up gardening. If you've never been on a boat, it is essential to discover how your system reacts.

If you are always seasick, then consider the circumstances. Think about what kind of boat you have been on. Some boats roll more than others and even the best boaters feel queasy. Ask yourself what you ate before you went out. Greasy foods or alcohol can contribute to seasickness. Some people have inner-ear problems and suffer from motion sickness. Find out what category you fit into. If you only get seasick in very windy and lumpy conditions, you can probably find a cure. If you get seasick walking down the dock, stay ashore and tend the roses.

The most important thing to recognize is that seasickness is real and that the symptoms can lead to serious problems. Seasickness should not be ignored, because vomiting will lead to dehydration. Small quantities of liquid should be drunk. Soda crackers or similar solids should be eaten as often as possible. Anyone with regular seasickness should avoid alcohol the night before the outing.

TIP
If you suffer from dehydration, get medical attention quickly.

Overcoming seasickness is largely a matter of your body's sensory system readjusting to being on water. Often this readjustment will take a day or two of continual time onboard. Because you usually live on land, your senses have to learn new patterns when you are on the water. First, try to get aboard the boat the night before you are going on a trip. That way you can sleep aboard and start to acclimate your system to being afloat. Watch what you eat before you head out. Eggs and bacon may be a wonderful breakfast on board, but not if you get seasick. Have some dry toast, a bagel, or a muffin. Avoid stimulants such as coffee or tea. You might also wish to discuss anti-nausea medication options with a healthcare professional.

CHAPTER 7

DECK GEAR

Y ou need sails to help make the boat go. You need an anchor, or anchors, to help make the boat stay in one place. And you need other gear to handle the sails and anchors. Those are the basics—but they aren't as simple as they sound.

COMMON SAIL TYPES

Sails today are made of various composites depending on the needs of the sailors and intended uses of the boat. Racers want the fastest low-stretch sail possible. Such sails may use Mylar, Kevlar, Spectra, carbon fibers and other high-strength materials. Be warned: they can be expensive. Cruisers want sails with high durability that are protected against ultraviolet degradation. Headsails on cruisers are usually stowed rolled up on the furling gear, which means that mildew resistance is important. Small-boat sailors also want high durability sails, but most small boats don't have roller-furling gear. This may make their sails stiffer and slightly more difficult to handle.

Sails are not flat like paper. They are very carefully cut and assembled so as to present a subtle aerofoil shape to get the maximum driving force and the minimum heeling for the wind strength. Boats with high stability tend to have slightly fuller sails (ones with more curvature) than boats with low stability. This gives the more stable boat more driving force.

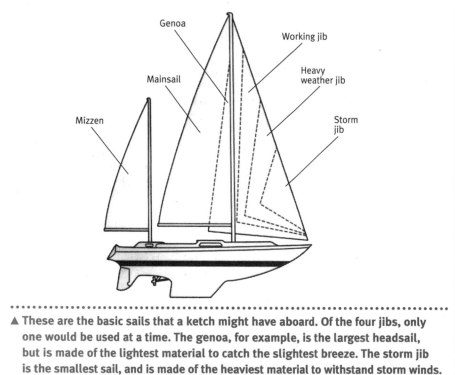

▲ These are the basic sails that a ketch might have aboard. Of the four jibs, only one would be used at a time. The genoa, for example, is the largest headsail, but is made of the lightest material to catch the slightest breeze. The storm jib is the smallest sail, and is made of the heaviest material to withstand storm winds.

Mainsail

This is the sail aft of the mast. While some mainsails are "loose footed" and attached only at the fore and aft corners, more often they are attached along the length of the boom either by a boltrope sewn into the sail or by slides. A cat rig has a single large mainsail.

Genoa

A large foresail attached to the forestay. Often larger than the mainsail, it is made of the lightest material to catch the slightest breeze. It is sometimes called a jenny.

Jib

A foresail attached to a jibstay. The working jib is smaller than the genoa, and the heavy weather jib is smaller still. The smallest sail, the storm jib, is made of the heaviest material to withstand storm winds. Only one jib is used at a time.

Staysail

The inner foresail (also known as a headsail) on a cutter, set inside the jib.

Mizzen

A small, light, triangular sail attached to the mizzenmast in the stern of a yawl or ketch.

Spinnaker

A three-sided, lightweight sail set in the bow of a boat. Spinnakers fill with wind when it is blowing from behind.

Standing rigging is the structure designed to keep the mast up and support the sails. It helps to think about each part of standing rigging as performing a particular function. On a single-spreader rig, as shown in the figure at right, the backstay and the forestay keep the head of the mast from moving around in a fore and aft direction. The headstay usually has the headsail set on it. (Stays support the mast fore and aft.) The upper shrouds also help to keep the masthead in place transversely. In general, shrouds are the wires that support the mast transversely. The spreaders help to spread the shrouds wider, so that the upper shrouds can be effective in holding the masthead in place. The vertical lower shroud is the extension of the upper shroud to the deck. The lower diagonal shrouds support the middle of the mast and stop it from moving about. Two forward lowers and two aft lowers form a square base to hold the middle of the mast in place. A single lower and a midstay forms a triangular base to hold the mast middle in place. Additional spreaders only mean that you will need to add extra shrouds in between the spreaders. Additional spreaders can make the mast thinner and more aerodynamically efficient. Of course, there's a trade-off. Thinner masts are harder to tune and harder to keep straight, so they are rarely used on cruising boats. Cruising boats use one or two spreaders and occasionally three, but rarely more.

> **☨ T I P**
>
> Fasten telltales to the shrouds to find out which way the wind is blowing. These strips of yarn or cloth stream away from the wind.

Standing rigging can take many forms, but mostly it is based on the number of spreaders a rig has. Single-spreader rigs are the easiest to tune and the easiest to set up. On boats with two headsails, the stays are often set up with a headstay and midstay, or a headstay, midstay, and babystay. This allows the headsail to be set on the headstay, a staysail to be set on the midstay, and the babystay to control the bend of the lower part of the mast.

On most racing and high performance cruising boats the shrouds are made of stainless steel solid rod, known as rod rigging. The rod rigging is best when it is discontinuous—connected to link plates at spreader ends rather than run across the end of the spreader to the masthead. Rod rigging stretches much less than the wire rigging used on most cruisers. Because of

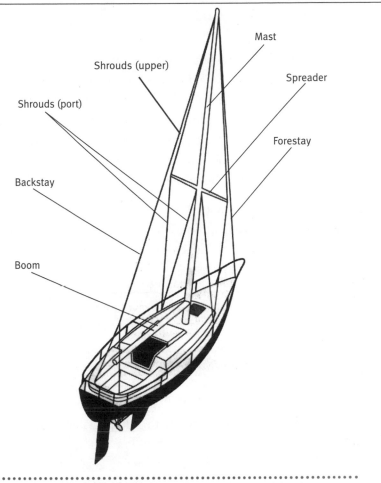

Mast

Shrouds (upper)

Spreader

Shrouds (port)

Forestay

Backstay

Boom

▲ **Standing rigging supports the mast against the tremendous strain imposed by the sails. This sailboat has upper and lower shrouds, a single forestay and a split backstay.**

the stretch characteristics many performance cruisers use rod shrouds, but have wire headstay and backstays to provide a little "give" to the rig when the boat is pounding to windward. On a classic cruiser all the stays and shrouds are made of 1 x 19 stainless steel wire.

On boats with two masts, the rigging should be set up so that both masts are independently supported. That way if one mast falls down for any reason, the other can be used to get you home.

Winches

On all but the smallest sailboats, winches are used to control sheets and raise halyards. The number of winches on board depends on the size of the boat and the number of lines. In general, boats that are about 22 feet long have two single-speed winches and a few cleats. Boats up to 30 feet may have four or six winches and a bank of lockoffs. Lockoffs allow a line to be taken to a winch to be wound in, then locked off or jammed. After it has been locked off, a line can be removed from the winch, leaving the winch free for other lines.

The power of winches is a function of the gear ratio and the power ratio. The gear ratio is the number of times you must run the handle to rotate the drum once, or:

$$\text{Gear ratio} = \frac{\text{number of handle revolutions}}{\text{number of drum revolutions}}$$

The power ratio is the gear ratio times the diameter of the circle described by the winch handle divided by the diameter of the drum, or:

$$\text{Power ratio} = \frac{\text{gear ratio x handle length x 2}}{\text{diameter of winch drum}}$$

If we have a three-speed winch with a drum diameter of 4.5 inches and a 10-inch handle, the gear ratio in first gear is 1; that is, the winch turns one revolution for each turn of the handle. In second gear, the winch handle turns five times for every drum revolution, so the gear ratio is 5. In third gear, it turns 12 times, so the gear ratio is 12.

In first gear, the power ratio of this winch is $\frac{1 \times (10 \times 2)}{4.5} = 4.44$

In second gear, it is: $\frac{5 \times (10 \times 2)}{4.5} = 22.22$

As you can see, the power ratio is the manufacturer's term for mechanical advantage. Manufacturers have carefully optimized their gear and power ratios so that sheets and guys can be pulled in most efficiently. Since the late 1970s most manufacturers have added self-tailing tops to their winches, which allows a single crewmember to turn the winch and reel the line in.

GROUND TACKLE

Ground tackle, as its name implies, is the gear used to attach the boat to the ground (seabed). It comprises the anchor, the anchor chain or line, the bow roller, a windlass or capstan, and a chain-claw or devil's-claw to hold the chain in place when the anchor is in use.

Anchors

There are many different kinds of anchors on the market, and manufacturers are adding more all the time. All that an anchor needs to do is hold the boat in place. To do this, it can either be heavy or it can dig into the bottom. Some anchors are a combination of both (plow and Navy anchors), in that they are heavy and they dig in. There is another type that literally screws into the seabed. For permanent moorings this is without a doubt the strongest of all. The following pages describe the most common types.

> The **holding power** of an anchor is a value given to it by the manufacturer, but in practice, holding power depends on many factors and can vary tremendously. For example, an anchor may not have the weight to penetrate a pebble bottom and may have little or no holding power in this situation. On the other hand, some anchors snag cable or debris on the ocean floor and cannot be pulled out. They have tremendous holding power in that situation. Holding power should be taken as an indication of an anchor's potential, not as a hard and fast fact. You may never achieve the holding power given by the manufacturer, but then again, you may exceed it many times—and never get your anchor back.

Danforth or fluke anchor

Developed in 1938 by R.D. Ogg and R. S. Danforth, the lightweight Danforth anchor is made of two flat steel or aluminum flukes that dig into the bottom of the sea or lakebed. It is especially effective in mud, sand, or clay, although it sometimes skips over rocky bottoms. This style of anchor is available from Fortress (you can adjust the fluke angle on the Fortress for better holding in soft mud), Simpson-Lawrence, and other manufacturers, now that the Danforth patent has expired. The foldable design makes it easy to stow and easy to use.

Plow anchor

The plow anchor was originally invented by Sir Geoffrey Taylor in the 1930s. He named it the CQR or "Secure" anchor, by which name it is sometimes known. It looks just like a plow, with a large, almost triangular fluke that pivots at the end of a shank. The fluke buries itself into soft bottoms and has excellent holding power. Because they're relatively heavy and bulky (the lightest start at 15 pounds), they are best for larger boats (25 feet or more.) They are usually stored on bow rollers. The Delta, a new plow-shaped anchor from Simpson-Lawrence, is made of one piece and has holding power similar to the regular plow.

Bruce anchor

This anchor was originally developed in Britain in the 1950s for use with offshore oil and gas drilling rigs. Scaled down for recreational use, it can right itself no matter how it lands on the bottom. It works well on mud, sand, or rocks.

Max anchor

The broad flukes of the Max anchor give it greater holding power. Since its shank is adjustable, the angle can be increased for soft bottoms.

The Fisherman anchor

The Fisherman anchor looks like the traditional anchor with upturned arms and small flukes, but it often goes by different names. If it has diamond-shaped flukes it might be called a Herreschoff anchor. With spear-shaped flukes it is known as the Nicholson anchor. The Yachtsman anchor has triangular flukes. It is useful for hard rocky bottoms or bottoms with lots of weeds or grass. It is heavier than a burying-type anchor.

Grapnel anchor

The grapnel or grappling anchor has five curved prongs around a central shank. It is best used on wrecks and should be considered to be a throwaway because it is very hard to retrieve once it has hooked the wreck. It can also be dragged along the bottom to retrieve lost anchor lines.

TIP

Remember: you must drop anchor whenever you stop for lunch, fishing, or scuba diving.

The following should be considered as mainly permanent, rather than temporary—put down or pulled up during the course of the cruise. But there are some exceptions.

Mushroom anchor

The mushroom anchor looks like an upside-down mushroom. Since it takes a long time to dig into the bottom, it should only be used on permanent moorings. For short periods of time in mud bottoms it can be used for inflatables, canoes, and rowboats which put a light strain on the anchor. Mushroom anchors that have been buried in the bottom may also used as part of a permanent mooring system.

Helix anchors

These anchors screw into the seabed and must be put in place by a diver. They require a bottom that will permit them to be screwed in until the eye on the end is just visible above the mud line. Because they are screwed in, Helix anchors have incredible holding power. In a hurricane in the Caribbean, a Helix anchor screwed in place by a diver on a large boat just before the storm hit is reputed to have held several boats while other boats and anchors were driven aground. Once the Helix anchor is in place it has little or no impact on the surrounding area.

The number of anchors you should carry depends upon several things— the size of your boat, whether it is used only in familiar, sheltered waters or cruises to many harbors, and to some extent, the type of anchors used. Note also that anchors need to be secured very tightly when the boat is at sea. Heavy anchors have been known to fly off their roller and stave-in bow planking as they swing around on the end of their chain.

Many boats carry two anchors, with the weight of the heavier one about $1\frac{1}{2}$ times the weight of the lighter one. For cruising boats, three are undoubtedly better. This allows for two anchors to be carried on deck—a light lunch hook for brief stops while someone is aboard, and a working anchor for ordinary service. The third might be a big, spare, storm anchor, which may be stowed below.

Fortress anchor

Fortress anchors are similar to Danforths with a few differences. Fortress anchors can be taken apart for easier stowage in their own bag. The angle of their fluke can be adjusted to enable the anchor dig in more deeply. At the most extreme angle, the flukes of a Fortress anchor can be set at 45 degrees for better holding power.

The Delta

A new plow-shaped anchor from Simpson-Lawrence, is made all of one piece and can be used instead of a plow or Danforth for mud, shale, sandy, and silt bottoms.

Kedge anchor

A kedge anchor is a small anchor used to warp the boat from one berth to another. But the name is commonly applied to any small anchor used for a short period of time.

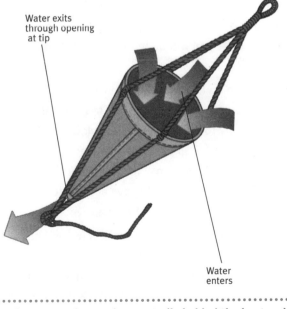

Water exits through opening at tip

Water enters

▲ A floating sea anchor, or drogue, trails behind the boat and slows it down. It is useful for anglers and sailors who want to keep their stem going straight ahead in rough seas.

Now that you have your anchor, you're almost ready to anchor your boat. **How much anchor line do you need?** Before you can figure that out, you'll need to have some idea of the areas in which you'll anchor and how much scope is required—that is, the length of anchor line you need to let out when compared to the depth of water.

Anchors are most secure when the angle of the anchor line is as close to the horizontal as possible. This may mean that you will have to pay out a huge amount of line. If you have chain near the anchor it serves to keep the anchor line nearly horizontal. Generally, depending on the conditions, you can use more or less scope, but the absolute minimum is about five to one. (That is, the anchor line is five times the water depth.) You might only use this scope if you were anchoring for lunch or for an afternoon swim. If you were to anchor overnight, the length of the rode should be five to seven times the depth. In heavy weather you may want to pay out ten times the depth or more on two anchors. Consequently, the length of your anchor line should be about ten times the depth of water where you will anchor. If you normally anchor in 40 feet of water, you'll find it easiest to have two 200-foot coils of anchor line. Most of the time only one coil will be in use, but you'll have the spare for emergencies.

An anchor line can be all chain, all nylon, or a combination of both. The best anchor lines are those that have two to three fathoms (12 to 18 feet) of chain shackled directly to the anchor and a nylon anchor line shackled to the chain. The chain keeps the anchor as near to horizontal as possible, while the nylon line provides some resiliency to the anchor line. In heavy seas a nylon line allows the boat to pitch and heave at the end of the line without the restrictions imposed by a heavy anchor chain.

Each shackle should be moused—that is, a wire should be passed through the shackle pin eye and wrapped around the shackle to prevent the pin from coming undone. See the table at right to decide on the ideal chain size for your boat. Mousing the pin will make it a little more difficult to get it around your windlass's chain gypsy, but it is safer in the long run. If your shackle pin comes undone, wave goodbye to your anchor.

STORM ANCHORS: RECOMMENDED SIZES			
Boat length ft (m)	Rode length ft (m)	Rode size in (mm)	Chain size* in (mm)
Up to 15 (4.6)	125 (38.1)	5/16 (8)	3/16 (5)
15 to 25 (4.6 to 7.6)	150 (45.7)	3/8 (10)	1/4 (6)
26 to 30 (7.9 to 9.1)	200 (61)	7/16 (11)	5/16 (8)
31 to 35 (9.4 to 10.6)	300 (91.4)	1/2 (13)	3/8 (10)
36 to 40 (10.9 to 12.1)	400 (121.9)	5/8 (16)	7/16 (11)
41 to 50 (12.5 to 15.2)	500 (152.4)	5/8 (16)	7/16 (11)
51 to 60 (15.5. to 18.3)	500 (152.4)	3/4 (18)	1/2 (12)

RECOMMENDED SIZES BY ANCHOR TYPE					
Boat length ft (m)	Fortress model no.	Plow lbs (kg)	Bruce lbs (kg)	Delta lbs (kg)	Danforth standard model
Up to 15 (4.6)	FX-7	6 (2.4)	4.4 (2)	9 (3.6)	8-S
15 to 25 (4.6 to 7.6)	FX-7	15 (6)	11 (5)	14 (5.7)	13-S
26 to 30 (7.9 to 9.1)	FX-11	25 (10.1)	16.5 (7.5)	22 (8.9)	22-S
31 to 35 (9.4 to 10.6)	FX-16	35 (14.1)	22 (10)	22 (8.9)	40-S
36 to 40 (10.9 to 12.1)	FX-23	45 (18.2)	33 (15)	35 (14.1)	65-S
41 to 50 (12.5 to 15.2)	FX-37	60 (24.2)	44 (20)	55 (22.2)	130-S
51 to 60 (15.5. to 18.3)	FX-55	75 (30.3)	66 (30)	55 (22.2)	180-S

*Recommended chain length: 1/2 foot of chain for each foot of boat length. Larger vessels should use an all-chain rode.

▲ The sizes above are recommended by manufacturers as suitable for use as storm anchors. For everyday anchoring in good to moderate weather, one size smaller can be used in most cases. All uses assume good holding ground; a scope of at least five to one in good weather, more in storms; and shelter from prevailing seas.

Nylon is the most popular material for anchor line. It's strong, long-lasting, and relatively cheap. Most important for anchoring, it's elastic, able to stretch from 15% to 25% of its original length. Make sure you buy marine-quality, three-strand nylon line rather than the less expensive non-marine nylon, which will stiffen and become hard to use after it has been immersed in salt water for a while. Three-strand nylon anchor line is laid by twisting three separate strands of nylon together. The only problem with nylon is that, because it stretches so much, it is prone to chafe and must be protected.

Davis Instruments and Perimeter Industries both make chafe-guards that protect nylon line quite well. At the other end, chafe is prevented by splicing the nylon around a thimble, through which the shackle is passed.

Another option is to buy braided Dacron line. This is not the double-braided line used for halyards, but a single-braided line that stretches up to 20%, rather like a plaited line. The best braided anchor line is made by New England Ropes in Fall River, MA. Dacron is a very strong material and does not chafe quite as badly as nylon.

Polypropylene should not be used as an anchor line. It tends to float and exerts an upward pull on the anchor.

Bow rollers

Another essential part of the anchor handling system is the bow roller. Anchor rollers help to keep the bow roller away from the hull and serve as a place to stow the anchor. The best bow rollers are made to suit specific anchors and allow the anchor to be pinned tightly through the roller. That way the anchor is unlikely to go AWOL if the chain slips.

To help figure out how much scope you have out, **mark that scope!** Spend a few hours over the winter marking your anchor line. You can either paint it at 1- or 2-fathom (6- or 12-feet) intervals up to 10 fathoms (60 feet). Then, at 5-fathom (30-feet) intervals you can splice brightly colored plastic markers through the anchor line.

Windlasses and capstans

A windlass has a horizontal axle and a capstan has a vertical axle, although the two names have become almost interchangeable. Windlasses and capstans should have a rope drum and a chain gypsy, as shown below. The rope drum is used to pull in the anchor line. The rope is then slid into the chain gypsy to secure the anchor tightly. This is a windlass for a larger boat, but many small boats use a low profile windlass. The low profile windlass poses special problems in that the nylon anchor line must be spliced right into the anchor chain so that it will go around the chain gypsy. Some low profile windlasses have a cut-out device to prevent the motor from overloading if undue strain is put on it. Sometimes this will happen when the anchor chain is only halfway in and you will have either to haul it in by hand or to wait until the rest kicks in and the windlass works again.

▲ This vertical windlass has a smooth drum for line over a gypsy one for chain; they can be operated independently. The anchor chain passes around the gypsy and through a deck opening to the chain locker. The smooth drum can be used for a second anchor, or for warping the vessel into a berth.

Other deck hardware includes cleats, hatches, tracks, dodgers, and possibly a bimini top. Each has an essential role to play on deck. Cleats, of which there are several types, make it easy to fasten lines. Hatches allow air and people to circulate throughout the boat. Tracks make it easy to adjust sails to improve their performance. Dodgers and bimini tops keep the rain and sun off you while you are using the boat.

Cleats

Cleats should be sized to suit the lines that will go around them. To find the best cleat size, multiply the diameter of the rope by sixteen. In other words, a half-inch rope is best on an 8-inch long cleat. Bow cleats should be one or two sizes larger to allow the boat to be towed.

Cam cleats work well for a time, but eventually the jaws get worn and the cleat slips. This is especially true of plastic cam cleats. Cam cleats should be selected from a chart given by the manufacturer.

Clam cleats hold the rope by using its tension to cause two cams to jam the cleat tightly. They are spring-loaded and eventually the springs deteriorate, but you can expect to get several years' use out of them.

Hatches

Hatches should be located in as many places as possible on deck. Hatches that people need to pass through should be a minimum of 324 square inches, or 18 inches on each side of the square. Smaller hatches should have screens over them to keep insects out. Foredeck hatches should open aft, so that an oncoming wave will slam the hatch shut. Hatches that open forward make it possible for an oncoming wave to go right below.

On many new boats the hatch tops are slippery plexiglass. A smart boat owner will place strips of non-skid across the glass to prevent crew from hurting themselves. Hatches should not leak, but poor installation often . causes leaks. Check at the sides and ends of hatches on used boats for leaks.

Tracks

Most boats have at least one headsail track down the side of the boat. When buying a used boat, you should check the track car pins and slide the car forward and aft to make sure it moves properly. Also look at the toerail to see if it has been distorted by high loads. When looking at tracks make sure that the sheets can be led to the winch without chafing on the coaming or rail.

On boats with good tracks, check to see that the sails can be sheeted to the tracks. If they can't, you may have to buy new sails or get the old ones recut. If the boat has more than one track on each side, make sure you check everything and that there are additional track cars available.

Dodgers and bimini tops

If you plan on going out when the weather is a little windy, you'll find that a dodger helps to keep the spray off the people in the cockpit. In stormy conditions it also gives you a place to shelter. If the boat has a dodger, try all the winches to make sure you can turn the handles under the dodger. Check from the helm to see what visibility is like over or through the dodger. Check to see if the dodger side or front windows can be raised. Raising them may be a godsend in calm, windless conditions.

With the current consciousness of the harm sun can cause, bimini tops, which shade the helmsman and most of the cockpit, are becoming very popular. Any bimini should be foldable so that it can be stowed if the boat has to sail to windward. It should not interfere with the boom or any of the operations of the boat and should be high enough that you can stand up under it, while remaining in the shade.

If you organize the deck gear carefully, there is no reason you should not be able to set and stow sails easily, handle the anchor with ease, tune the rig properly, and enjoy the deck of your new boat.

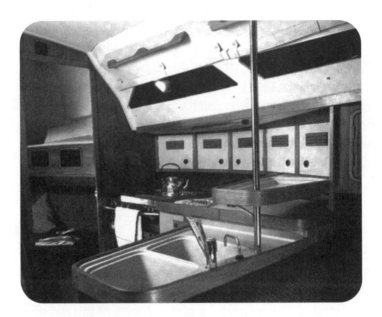

CHAPTER 8

INSIDE THE BOAT

There are a number of features that you may want in your boat. In the galley, you'll want a stove that will allow you to do the type of cooking you are used to. You may desire a shower, or a large sink, or even a bidet. You may also want a lot of storage space, a workshop, bookshelves, and a comfortable navigation area. All these features must be fitted into the interior.

Below Deck

On smaller boats, there may not be very much space for a galley. You may have to resort to a single burner butane-powered stove and an ice chest. However, by shuffling a couple of pans back and forth, it is possible to cook eggs and bacon for breakfast on a single burner. While the crew is eating their breakfast, you can put the water on for coffee.

The galley: the heart of the boat

On boats up to about 40 feet, the galley may include a large refrigerator, a stove with up to four burners, an oven, twin sinks, storage space for food and crockery, and a cutting board with a cutlery drawer. All the comforts of home, but on a limited scale. On cruising boats over 40 feet long, the galley may have all the items that you would find at home, and on boats with a generator, there may even be 110-volt outlets that allow you to run your coffeemaker, toaster, and Cuisinart.

When comparing the galleys of similar boats it's helpful to measure the amount of usable countertop space, the size and depth of the sink, and the volume of the dry-storage compartments. Look for special touches such as slide-away cutting boards and slide-out food bins. They show that the builder has put extra thought into making the galley more efficient.

▲ A deluxe galley with all the comforts of home.

Here's a checklist of what to look for in the galley.

✔ A location that keeps the cook out of the way of the rest of the crew.

✔ A layout that can be used safely when the boat is heeled on either tack.

✔ Anti-skid footing for the cook.

✔ Places for the cook to balance, hold on, and attach a harness.

✔ A strong bar in front of the stove.

✔ A stove fitted with gimbals so that it can pivot 35 degrees or more on each tack.

✔ A lock so that the stove can be held flat when in harbor.

✔ Fixtures that prevent the stove from jumping out of the gimbals if the boat should be inverted.

✔ Secure spots where utensils and dishes can be held at meal times. (Usually the top of the stove is the only level place when at sea.)

✔ A dishwashing and drying arrangement. If you go offshore the galley should have a saltwater intake for rinsing dishes.

✔ Drawers, doors, cupboards, and top-opening lockers that will not spring open in rough weather.

✔ A drawer for galley knives. Do not use knife slots, as they will allow knives to jump out if the boat gets hit by a large wave.

✔ Adequate countertop area for food preparation.

✔ A stove big enough for your needs. Make sure you have enough burners, a broiler, and an oven large enough to accommodate your favorite baking and roasting pans.

✔ Pot and pan stowage that is both adequate and accessible.

✔ Countertops that have strong, high fiddle rails (3 to 4 inches) for containing cookware and dishes when the boat heels or rolls.

✔ Adequate ventilation. At the very least, you should have one opening port and one opening hatch over the stove. A Nicro SolarVent is also a good feature to have in the deckhead over the stove.

On smaller boats, cups and dishes will probably be plastic or paper. On larger boats, china and glassware may be used just like at home. The shelves where dishes and glasses are stored should have partitions to keep the crockery separate and stop it from banging together.

The Stove

Most marine stoves use either alcohol, kerosene, electricity, liquified petro-leum gas (LPG), or compressed natural gas (CNG). The 2- or 3-burner alcohol stove is most common on small boats under 26 feet long. Care must be taken with alcohol stoves when refilling the stove. Alcohol is easily ignited and the flaming alcohol can run everywhere as the boat rolls. LPG or propane is the most common type of fuel for a marine stove. Any boat with a propane sys-tem should have a gas detector system because propane is heavier than air and will lie in the bilges of the boat. Compressed natural gas is lighter than air but does not have the BTU capacity of propane. (It will take longer to boil water.) Gas stoves should also have a turn-off switch near the stove in addi-tion to the stove controls. When not in use, most experts recommend that propane stoves be turned off at the tank for additional safety.

A propane tank should be installed in its own locker, which, according to the U.S. Coast Guard regulations, must be vented over the side. You should not stow anything other than propane in the propane locker. Heavier objects bouncing around in the locker have been known to damage the propane tank and line.

Kerosene is not often used because pressurizing and operating a kerosene stove is not all that easy. It can also be difficult to find kerosene that burns cleanly.

Electricity is probably the safest source of energy aboard a boat, but an auxiliary generating plant is required to produce the large amounts of AC power required. Typically, a two-burner electric stove requires about 1500 watts of power, and a four-burner about 3500 watts.

Sailboat stoves should be gimbaled to about 35 degrees either side of vertical. They should also have a lock-ing device so that the stove can be fixed in place. The Ocean Racing Council (ORC) requires that all stoves on boats be engineered to avoid the stove jumping out of the gimbals even when the boat is inverted.

> **TIP**
>
> Install ground fault circuit interrupters (GFCIs) into your electrical systems to ground random electrical currents before they find another conduc-tor—like you.

If you plan to cook onboard regularly, you should look for a stove with three or four burners and an oven. When inspecting the stove, open the oven to see if the stove tips forward when the door is opened. If it does, you will have to remember to remove pots on the stove top before opening the door or they may fall on you.

Stoves should also have space alongside them to allow the cook to stand to one side of the stove. That way, if a pot falls off the stovetop the cook is clear. There should also be a strong bar across the front of the stove to prevent the cook from falling into it. There should be strong padeyes to one side of the stove to help hold the cook (wearing a harness) in place if the boat is to go offshore. Finally, all stoves should have deep fiddle rails to hold pots and pans in place.

Microwaves

Microwaves provide an efficient alternative to the conventional stove (provided that you have a source for 110-volt power). They reduce cooking time, power consumption, and the amount of heat released into the cabin. Microwaves can heat water quickly and cook many foods. Most owners install ordinary 110-volt household microwaves on their boats and power them with an inverter, shore supply, or an onboard genset. Although there are 12-volt marine and trucking microwave ovens on the market, they are a little more expensive than the household units and are slightly smaller.

Inverter

If you wish to use your 110-volt microwave when the engine is turned off, you could use an inverter. An inverter turns 12- or 24-volt battery power into 110 volts to drive household appliances such as TVs or hairdryers. Inverters should be thought of as using high power for a short time or low power for a longer time. They should not be used at high power for a long time as this will drain the batteries completely.

Refrigeration

The method used to keep food and drinks cool will vary from boat to boat. Boats under about 25 feet generally have a portable ice chest that can be filled at home and loaded on board the boat. Boats between 25 and 40 feet may have an insulated icebox or compressor-driven refrigeration in a built-in ice box. Boats over 40 feet may have a built-in freezer in addition to the icebox. Boats over sixty feet may use commercial freezers or refrigerators.

If you have an icebox, you should check the opening to make sure that you can get a large block of ice through it. Solid ice takes longer to break down than the kind of ice cubes you buy in the supermarket.

If the boat has a built-in unit, the insulation should be as thick as possible. The thicker the insulation, the longer the ice will last. Insulation should be thicker against the hull of the boat, where water temperature may be in the 70s or higher.

If your refrigerator is driven by a compressor, make sure that it uses R-12 (sometimes known as freon-12 or dichlorodifluoromethane) or one of the other non-ozone-depleting gases. Freon has been banned because it is a danger to the ozone layer. If your boat does not have a generator, you will have to run the main engine in order to bring the temperature of the refrigeration unit down. Usually, you will need to run your engine for about an hour each day to keep the icebox or cooler cold.

Marine toilet or "the head"

The term "head" comes from the days of old-time sailing ships when the toilets were in the forward part of the boat, on either side of the bowsprit. While heads have moved into a more comfortable part of the boat, they are still required on all but the smallest boats. Small boats under about 28 feet usually have a portable marine toilet, such as a Porta Potti. This type of toilet is used on board, taken ashore at the end of the day, and emptied in your home toilet or at a pump-out station.

TIP
On small boats, try a portable marine head—or Porta Potti.

Larger boats up to about 45 feet usually have pump toilets. These marine toilets require you to pump seawater through them to flush. Because of the increase in no-discharge zones, most marine toilets empty into holding tanks, and are pumped out at pump-out stations in the local marina.

TIP
Clean the head after each trip with a commercial toilet cleaner.

On boats over 45 feet, various strategies are used to macerate or incinerate waste matter and store it in a holding tank. The new head from Wilcox-Crittenden, called Silent-Flush, is part of the revolution sweeping the marine toilet business. This unit is flushed by pushing a button and is almost silent.

The shower

In addition to the head, marine toilet compartments should have a washbasin or sink, some storage space for towels, soaps, and paper, and, on boats over 30 feet, a shower. On boats from 28 to about 36 feet, the shower is usually part of the toilet compartment. This means that you may have to sit on the toilet and wrap a plastic shower curtain around you to take a shower. On larger boats, the shower compartment is a separate space at least 30 inches by 30 inches. If it is much smaller than that, you will have a hard time reaching all parts of your body. The showerhead in such a unit is known as a telephone shower and is moveable to allow you to rinse your entire body.

TIP
Keep a bar of seawater soap aboard, just in case.

Storage space

Boats need to have lots of storage space. When you go on board for the first time, you will probably bring casual clothes, sandals or sailing shoes, towels, and loads of other equipment. All these items will need to be stowed. Unless your boat is over about 40 feet, you will not have enough space to stow everything and will have to compromise. For example, on a 24-footer with three or four crew, sleeping overnight often entails tossing everyone's seabag into the nearest open floor space to ensure that all the crewmembers have a bunk. The next day, the bunks are filled with seabags while the crew sails.

In the galley you'll want to stow food, and if space is at a premium, the cook often uses other unusual spaces. For example, canned goods are often stowed in the bilge. For a long trip extra bread may be stowed in all manner of places, even the head. In general, stow heavy stuff low and light stuff high to increase the boat's stability.

⚓ T I P

If stowing canned goods in the bilge, remove paper labels and use a magic marker to name the contents. Paper label rot and drop off.

Ventilation

Ventilation should be adequate throughout the boat without the need to open hatches. A boat that is left at the marina or dock for a week should have some method of automatically circulating air throughout the hull. Usually this means several vents on the side of the cabin or on the cabin top. Circulating air keeps the boat smelling fresh and helps to prevent mildew. If the boat is locked up tight all week, you will find that stale odors, mildew, and rot will start fairly quickly. During bright sunny days the interior temperature of your boat may routinely exceed a hundred and twenty degrees. If you leave food or drinks onboard, high temperatures will probably spoil them.

Bunks

Bunks should be at least 6 feet 4 inches long and about 28 to 30 inches wide. In a warm weather harbor, the largest bunk seems too small, but in a storm you'll want the smallest bunk possible to keep you wedged in place. Bunks can taper to about 16 inches at the foot, but if the bunk is near the aft corner of the boat (on the quarter) you may find that you are tipped downwards if you try to sleep on the lee side. In that case, switching ends is often helpful, but the bunk foot needs to be larger than 18 inches.

The most comfortable bunks are in the middle of the boat, but usually they are settee berths and must be converted from a settee for daytime use to a bunk for nighttime use. Seating is generally about 16 to 18 inches wide, but a bunk needs to be wider, so there is usually a method of making the bunk convert easily. Often, removing the seatback is all that is needed. In other cases a transom or drawer-like pull-out does the job. If you are looking at a boat that has convertible settee/bunks, make sure that they do both jobs well.

In the forward part of most sailboats are the vee-berths. In most cases, these bunks are only useable in harbor. The pitching motion of the boat as it moves through the waves makes them untenable in anything other than the calmest seas. If you plan to sleep two people in the vee berth, try before you buy. Quite often, vee berths measure 6 feet or less on the diagonal and may be smaller from top to bottom.

CHAPTER 9

NAVIGATION AND ELECTRONIC AIDS

Today's sailors should not depend on all the sophisticated electronic aids to help keep in touch with the rest of the world, but should have backup systems if they intend to go out of sight of land for any length of time. In general, you can use electronic navigation equipment such as a Global Positioning System, plotter, or electronic charts, but you should always have a backup plan.

The old-fashioned, tried-and-true hand navigation tools are a must, and you should know how to use them. A compass that has been adjusted properly, charts, parallel rules, and a sharp pencil will get you to most harbors safely and quickly. A book of tide and current tables, a hand bearing compass, and a keen eye will be all that you require on most trips. You should learn to navigate using these old-fashioned methods before you invest in electronic equipment.

⚓ TIP

For waterway guides and chart kits by area, call the Better Boating Association (781-982-4060); Waterway Guides (770-955-2500); or Embassy Boating Guides (888-839-5551)

Compass and charts

The most essential tool on any sailboat is still a compass. A compass determines direction by means of a freely rotating needle indicating magnetic north. A compass card, labeled with geographic directions, is mounted inside the compass. Your compass should be mounted directly on the pedestal or within easy sight of the helmsman. The lubber line—a dark line on the compass dome—should be aligned with the fore and aft centerline of the boat.

⚓ TIP

Don't look at the compass all the time as you steer a "compass course." Get your directional bearing and then steer toward a landmark straight ahead.

The markings on the cards should be large and simple enough to be readable in bad weather and through spray or mist. The larger the compass, the easier it will be to read (and the more expensive it will probably be). The compass should also have a red light and a dimmer switch for use at night.

A compass and charts are still required equipment aboard every boat, and no experienced boater would go to sea without studying a chart first. Marine charts are made by the U.S. National Oceanic and Atmospheric

Make sure you **swing your boat's compass** as soon as you take possession of it. If the compass was swung by the previous owner and you have moved the boat to a new area, have it swung properly. The earth's magnetic field is not consistent from coast to coast. An inaccurate compass can take you miles off course, and in fog you might go aground rather than into the harbor.

Administration (NOAA). They show water depth, the shape of land masses, latitude and longitude, and location of navigational markers. The first chart you should buy is U.S. Chart I. It tells you what all the symbols on all the other charts mean.

It is important to note that while your compass will point to magnetic north, the chart will indicate geographic north. That's because magnetic north is not true north on most points on the globe. The difference between the two is called variation. There is as much as 20 degrees variation along the northern coasts of Maine and Washington. If you are traveling long distances and navigating by compass, you will want to know how many degrees you should add or subtract to your course to compensate for the degree of variation in a given area.

COMPASS CRITERIA

When shopping for a compass, choose a quality instrument. Consider the points listed below. Remember that your compass is the most important navigational tool aboard your boat. **This is no place to cut corners.**

1. Can the compass be mounted in a location on your boat that allows for comfortable viewing for long periods of time?

2. Is the card easily read and appropriately marked?

3. Does the card remain level? It should not stick through reasonable levels of pitch and roll.

4. Does the card move uniformly through any course change?

5. Is the card "dead-beat?" That is, does it swing only once to a steady position?

6. Are there built-in compensating magnets?

7. Is there provision for night lighting, preferably with a dimmer?

8. Is the dome hemispherically shaped rather than flat?

9. Are the card and lubber's line fully gimbaled? Internal gimbals are best.

10. Is there a metal or rubber expansion chamber to allow for temperature changes?

11. Is there any significant parallax error when the compass is viewed from the side as compared to the rear?

LORAN

For about fifty years, the Long Range Navigation System (LORAN) was the prime electronic navigation system for the United States and Canada. The Global Positioning System has replaced it as the system of choice. But if you buy an older boat, you may find it still equipped with LORAN. In fact, many anglers prefer it for its repeatable accuracy. Loran utilizes a network of shore-based radio transmitters that are grouped in "chains." These chains are designed to provide accurate navigational fixes within 50 nautical miles from shore or out to the 100-fathom curve, whichever is greater. The U.S. government, which has maintained the system, is gradually phasing it out. Within the next two decades, it will probably be completely replaced by GPS.

The Global Positioning System (GPS)

The Global Positioning System is an advanced worldwide satellite navigation system designed and operated by the U.S. Department of Defense. It relies on signals transmitted from a group of 24 orbiting satellites. A GPS receiver determines vessel position by taking virtually instantaneous readings from at least three satellites (the latest receivers are 12-channel units that can "see" up to 12 satellites). The receiver calculates the vessel's position as the point at which the three spheres projected from each satellite intersect. It can tell you the speed, course, and latitude and longitude of your boat. But this information is only available after your boat has established a "history." In other words, the GPS receiver saves information about where you were a few minutes ago and compares that to your present location. The result is the course you were on a few minutes or seconds earlier. GPS units do not tell you where you will be in the future.

GPS units

GPS units come in either console-mounted or hand-held models. They are relatively inexpensive and getting cheaper all the time. The fixed units cost around $200, and the portable units are under $100. They're the most sophisticated navigational devices in the world, and every boat owner should have one. Even the least expensive ones come with navaids already loaded in, while on more expensive units you can load charts, street maps, and contours of your local area.

The latest GPS units can display buoys, cities, and streets, and can be used for navigation on board your boat or to get you home overland after your boating trip. To increase the repeatable accuracy of GPS, many manufacturers are adding in a feature known as Differential GPS (DGPS). DGPS uses radio waves in a manner similar to LORAN, and uses them to increase the accuracy of the GPS location. While Differential was originally used to replace the government installed Selective Availability (SA), it has come into its own now that SA has been turned off.

Chart plotters

A chart plotter shows a chart of the area in which you are sailing and locates your boat on that chart by means of the GPS signal. Chart plotters can be mounted in the cockpit, and some are available with daylight viewable screens. (In the past the biggest problem with plotters has been that the LCD screen "disappears" in bright sunlight.) Some daylight viewable screens are about the size of a laptop computer screen and can be used to plot your course before you set out. When you have plotted your course, you can link the plotter to the autopilot and, in theory, the boat will sail to its destination. When this system is linked to wind instruments in a complete system, such as the one available from RayMarine, the boat can sail to windward on autopilot.

Chart plotters are one of the most popular electronic gizmos ever to come along. With a chart plotter installed at your helm station, you can see your boat's track on the screen as it moves along. Before you go on your trip you can lay out a course, store waypoints, and calculate how long and how far it is to your destination. When you start on your trip you can plug in the autopilot and have the autopilot/GPS/plotter combination take you to your destination. Chart plotters can use an internal or external GPS input, display buoys, charts, navaids, and city streets, and some (depending on the software used) can tell you where the local chandlery or restaurants are when you come to a port.

Depth finders

Depth finders (also known as Fathometers) use an echo-ranging pulse to determine the distance between the hull of your boat and the sea bottom. They will help keep you out of shallow water and can also help you determine your position in a dense fog by enabling you to compare the depth on the finder with the depth recorded on the chart. The most inexpensive units, digital depth finders, show the depth in numbers displayed on a screen. Most popular, however, are the LCD screen displays, which show the bottom of the sea visually, including the fish swimming beneath the boat. LCD displays are invaluable to anglers, and a source of delight to kids.

Fish finders

If you are a truly dedicated fisherman you might want to look into a colored fish finder. These daylight-visible, colored LCD display screens show the contours of the seabed and also show any fish that get between the fish finder and the seabed. Generally, the fish shows up as a different color on the screen. Companies such as RayMarine make fish finders that can be linked to your GPS to bring you back to the same area every time.

Radar

Radar has a unique advantage in navigation in that a single instrument can measure both direction and distance. Radar can almost always make a measurement of direction despite fog, light rain, or darkness. Even small boats can have some of the latest LCD display radar sets. The latest radars integrate GPS location, and have overlays of charts to enable you to determine exactly where you are in relation to your chart, the shoreline, and any moving objects in the water.

Even more than other piloting methods, radar requires considerable practice and experience. Develop your radar procedures during fair weather and good conditions so that they are readily available in difficult circumstances and you can use them with confidence.

Electronic charts

Electronic charts are the most important part of plotter and GPS displays. There are a number of electronic chart manufacturers but the only ones used in plotters are vector charts made by C-Map or Navionics.

Understanding electronic charts

There are two types of electronic charts: raster and vector. Raster charts are paper charts that have been scanned into a computer. By adjusting for scale and data, most of the electronic chart programs seamlessly integrate raster charts into one master chart. With raster charts you see the same amount of detail whether you have zoomed in or out to the maximum.

Vector charts, on the other hand, are raster charts that have been reprogrammed so that each depth (or height) contour and each set of navaids are on different layers of the chart. This means that if you zoom out to the largest scale you will see outlines of continents and a few depth contours. As you keep zooming in, more detail reveals itself, until you can see each slip in a marina. Vector charts often incorporate more details than can be found on raster charts. For instance, some charts have a database of marinas, restaurants, repair shops, and other pertinent information that can be turned off or on at will.

Don't confuse electronic charts with navigation programs. Electronic charts allow you to do exactly what you do with a paper chart without a pencil or parallel rules. Electronic navigation programs allow you to utilize electronic charts in the same way a pencil, parallel rules, and a compass allow you to use a paper chart. Over and above that, electronic charts have some extra features. For example, instead of looking up tide tables, you can turn on the tide table overlay and see the tide arrows. If you animate the sequence, you can watch the tide change over the course of your trip.

To use an electronic navigation program, first zoom out until you can see your starting point and destination. Plot your course from one to the other without worrying if you cut across a bit of land. Now zoom in and add waypoints to insert the details of your course. Make sure that you go around the hard stuff leaving plenty of water around reefs, wrecks, and other shallow spots. Once the course information has been input (you can do this in an evening on your home computer) you can check the tide situation against your departure time, modify it if necessary, and save the entire program. For example, if you are leaving Long Island Sound's eastern end, you must go through one of three exits: Fisher's Island Sound, the Race, or the Gut. As the tide roars through these places at up to six knots, you need to plan your trip so that you will arrive at the Race or the Gut when the tide is going with you. To figure this out manually can be a tedious process, but by using an electronic chart program, you can do it in a few minutes.

On an electronic chart program you can also project where your boat will be in five or ten minutes, put a "hazard" ring around the boat—if the ring touches a hazard such as a wreck buoy, it sounds an alarm—or turn on or off the depth arrows so you know what depth of water you are sailing in. With the very latest programs you can access the program maker's website, download weather information for your area, and get a feel for wind direction and strength.

W herever you are on the water, you will want to be able to contact the rest of the world. Maybe you want to find out what a cloud buildup portends, or to let someone know where you are, or find out if someone will meet the boat when you arrive. If you're within 20 miles of land, a cell phone is the most convenient way to contact other people, but you have to remember to keep the phone charged. However, you should not use a cell phone to call for help or assistance unless you have no other method. The U.S. Coast Guard (USCG) cannot determine where the call originates. A cell phone signal might be relayed through a satellite dish in New Jersey while you are in Maine. Consequently, the USCG cannot triangulate where you are if you are not able to give a precise location.

Very High Frequency (VHF) radio

At longer distances with ranges up to thirty miles, depending on the height of the antenna, the top communications gear is VHF radio. The transmissions are basically line-of-sight, so if you are low down in a dinghy, you may only have a range of three miles. VHF signals are not reflected by the atmosphere, nor do they bend around the curvature of the earth.

The most important use of the VHF radio is safety. Anyone who has a radio turned on is required by law to monitor Channel 16 when not actually engaged on another channel. Channel 16 is the only channel to be used for distress calls and messages. It is the channel you would use if it were ever necessary to broadcast the Mayday call, signaling the danger of loss of life or vessel. The USCG also monitors this channel. Channel 16 is also used to establish contact with other boats, but only in order to agree on which working channel you will switch to. No non-emergency transmission on Channel 16 may exceed 30 seconds.

⚓ **T I P**

One great thing about VHF: it's free once you buy the equipment.

In order to lessen the congestion on Channel 16, the Federal Communications Commission has authorized the voluntary use of Channel 09 by non-commercial vessels for calling each other. Maintaining a watch for calls on Channel 09, however, may result in missing warnings and announcements from USCG stations and marine operators.

In order to minimize transmission time, VHF calls follow a standard operating procedure. (Operators use the boats' names.) A typical conversation would proceed as follows:

"Happy Day. . .Happy Day, this is Red Bird, over."

"Red Bird, this is Happy Day."

"Happy Day, this is Red Bird. Switch to six-eight."

"Roger, Red Bird. This is Happy Day. Roger six-eight."

(Both stations retune to Channel 68).

At the end of the call:

"Happy Day, out."

"Red Bird, out."

Console-mounted VHF radios cost about $100 to $500 as do hand-held VHF units, which are approximately the same size as a cell phone. Portable units are useful as a backup for a regular radio and in small oats with no installed radio system. However, they have limited output power and their antennae are much shorter and less efficient than larger models. As a result, they are unsuitable for anything more than relatively close communication.

For distances longer than 25 or 30 miles, single sideband (SSB) radio transmitters are used. These radios can send signals to relaying communications satellites. A vessel cannot be licensed for SSB radiotelephone unless it is already equipped with a VHF set, and it is required to try to communicate via VHF before using the lower and crowded frequencies of the SSB. Installation of SSB equipment usually requires the services of a trained and licensed technician. Unlike VHF radio, SSB requires a large "ground plane" of copper mesh panel in order to radiate its signals, and the panel needs to be installed.

EPIRB

Every boat that goes offshore beyond reliable VHF radio range—roughly 20 miles—should carry an Emergency Position-Indicating Radio Beacon (EPIRB). First-generation EPIRBs, operating on the 121.5 Mhz band and divided into Class A and Class B, operate on the emergency channels for civilian planes and the "guard" channel for military aircraft. When one or more of these detect the tone signal of an EPIRB, search and rescue activities begin. Unfortunately, first-generation EPIRBs suffer from voice-communication interference and the units have a very high incidence of false alarms. By some counts, over 90% of calls are false alarms.

Much more reliable are the second-generation EPIRBs that operate on the 406.5 Mhz band and use a dedicated frequency that is free of interference from other communications. Beacon signals are picked up by orbiting satellites. At $800 to $1,400, they are considerably more expensive than the first-generation equipment, but their far greater effectiveness makes them worthwhile. Some units can be interfaced to a GPS receiver and locate a distress location to an accuracy of less than a half mile. At close to $2,000, they are even more expensive. Once any EPIRB is activated in an emergency, it must be left on. To turn it off "to save the battery" severely disrupts rescue operations.

The latest development in EPIRB technology is to link the EPIRB to a GPS unit. This unit transmits the GPS location of the unit and can cut rescue time to a matter of minutes instead of hours or days.

 CHAPTER 10

BE PREPARED

A s skipper, you are responsible for the well-being of your sailboat and of everyone on board. You need to be as self-sufficient as possible on the water, which means having everything from tool and first-aid kits to life rafts.

Keeping a toolbox at sea is a special challenge. Even if your tools don't get wet, they are liable to rust in the salt air and spray. Some manufacturers do make special nickel cadmium tools for use on boats, but these are more expensive than regular tools. If you don't want to make the extra investment, you will have to take other precautions. These will include storing your tools in a watertight kit and storing the kit in a dry-storage box. Every time you use a tool, rub it clean with an oiled rag to prevent corrosion. You can also use a product such as Bulldog, a rust inhibitor that will protect your tools while they sit in the kit.

Here are some of the most basic, must-have tools:

- ► Blunt, needle-nosed, tapered, and electrical pliers
- ► Adjustable crescent and torque wrenches
- ► Sets of metric and English box, hex, and socket wrenches
- ► Flat screwdrivers, including one with an extra-long shaft for those hard-to-reach places
- ► Phillips-head screwdrivers
- ► Hammers
- ► Vise grips
- ► Sockets
- ► Bolt-cutters
- ► Hand drill and bits
- ► Axe
- ► C-clamps
- ► Small brushes
- ► Tap and die set
- ► Pry and crowbars
- ► Wire cutter
- ► Hacksaw
- ► Last but not least, a magnetic "wand" for retrieving bolts and other small tools that fall into the bilge.

TIP

Use sailing gloves to work the lines in windy weather. They'll prevent line burn.

Leaks and tears

You'll need an assortment of items to patch holes and control leaks. Duct tape has a million uses, from fixing a hose to sealing a bag. Marine sealer and super glue will help you stick just about anything together, including yourself.

If your boat starts to leak, it's probably because of damage to through-hull fittings and related parts such as hoses and keel bolts. You should have softwood plugs on board—one of appropriate diameter for each size of hull fitting on your boat. You can drive the plugs into place from the inside. Also keep on board underwater epoxy putty and rags for stuffing cracks. Perimeter Industries makes the Navirex Emergency Hull Repair Kit. This kit includes a sponge, plastic gloves, and a two-part resin/sealer. If your boat is holed, you mix the sealer in the lid of the box, soak the sponge in it, and then, wearing the gloves, ram the sponge into the hole. The entire mess sets up in a few minutes and you have a temporary patch.

Bring aboard a sail repair kit, which should include the following: needles, hanks, slides, grommets, battens, grommet tool, fids for braided line, sail cloth, Pressure Sensitive Adhesive (PSA, otherwise known as ripstop) tape, and sail palm.

Go through your boat and check what size nuts, bolts, screws, and washers are most prevalent and bring a few of each. Add in extra fuses, insulating electrical tape, insulated wire, and stainless steel hose clamps in the most common sizes. When deciding what to bring, ask yourself, "Can I get home without it?" If the answer is yes, leave it ashore. There is no sense in weighing your boat down with gear you may never use. In addition, you'll need spare winch equipment: bearings, pawls, snap rings, and grease. For onboard pumps, you'll need spare diaphragms, valves, gaskets, and hoses. Swiss army knives or one of the common multi-tools are always useful, too.

TIP
Make sure you have spare batteries for all your flashlights.

Finally, you'll need a flashlight, or rather, a few flashlights, because you can never have too many. Get some wide-beam lights that can illuminate the entire deck, some narrow beam lights to check your watch, or an instrument with a good spotlight that can pick up a mooring buoy or piling when you are approaching on a dark night.

You should always carry enough gear so that you'll be able to get your engine going even if it breaks down far from shore. Most sailors can sail their boats home if there is a problem with the engine. The only time there is likely to be a problem is if you are on a long trip, the engine dies, and you have no way to recharge the batteries or keep the refrigerator cool. Smart, mechanically inclined sailors will carry spare hoses, belts, and possibly an engine repair kit. But if you have no engine knowledge or are a klutz with all things mechanical, make sure your towing membership is paid up and hope for the best.

TIP

Is your auxiliary engine too noisy? Insulate it by adding high-density foam sheets to the inside of your engine box.

▲ The best precaution against an emergency is a well-maintained boat. Check your engines, batteries (as shown above), and all other systems regularly.

Caring for your skin

Although a deep suntan was once considered fashionable or healthy, today's medical recommendations warn about the dangers of chronic overexposure to the sun. Medical research shows that too much ultraviolet radiation not only causes skin to age prematurely, but may cause skin cancer to develop. Since boating involves hours on end in the sun, you can minimize your risk by taking the following precautions and by stocking your boat with the following:

✔ Protect your skin with good-quality commercial sunscreen that protects from both ultraviolet alpha (UVA) and ultraviolet beta (UVB) rays. The American Academy of Dermatology recommends year-round sun protection for everyone, and especially for fair-skinned people and those who burn easily. The Food and Drug Administration recognizes Sun Protection Factor (SPF) values between 2 and 15. It has not been determined whether sunscreens with SPF ratings over 15 provide additional protection.

> ⚓ **T I P**
> Remember: even on cloudy days, water, sand, and other surfaces reflect light that can burn severely.

✔ Apply sunscreen 15 to 30 minutes before exposure to the sun, and reapply often (every 60 to 90 minutes). Have a stash of sunscreen onboard, as you'll go through a lot of it. Kids on board? Be sure to carry sunscreen made especially for children, whose skin is more sensitive. Swimmers should use sunscreens labeled "water-resistant" and reapply as prescribed on the label.

✔ Wear UV-blocking wrap-around sunglasses. According to the American Red Cross, opthalmologists recommend sunglasses that have a UV absorption rate of 90 percent or above. Attach holders to your sunglasses, such as those made by Croakies or Chum's, to keep your sunglasses on. Also attach a "floater" to your glasses, just in case they do fall off in the water. Ask your eye doctor if you need prescription sunglasses.

✔ Exposure to the sun between the hours of 10 AM and 2 PM is the most harmful. Select clothing that minimizes your exposure to the sun, such as a wide-brimmed hat or visor, long-sleeved shirts, and long pants.

First aid kit

On shore, emergency medical assistance is usually just minutes away. But on the water, you are on your own—for a time, at least. Your confidence and competence in handling medical emergencies should be on a par with your seamanship skills. That confidence comes from knowledge and practice; both can be acquired and honed by basic and advanced first-aid courses.

In addition to at least one comprehensive first-aid manual, your boat should be equipped with a first-aid kit designed specifically for your needs. Day and weekend boaters, for example, need a kit stocked with basics, such as:

- Thermometer
- Tweezers
- Alcohol
- Sunscreen
- Scissors
- Bandages (plastic and cloth, assorted sizes)

- Gauze
- Aspirin
- Antibiotic cream or gel
- Eye-washing cup
- Hot water bottle/ice bag

Depending on the cruising waters and the crew members aboard, you might also want to stock items such a remedies for seasickness and jellyfish stings. Long-range cruisers require more extensive first-aid supplies and lifesaving equipment as well as a wide range of medications. In order to reduce the care-giver's risk of infection, every first-aid kit should also include a waterless antiseptic hand cleaner and disposable gloves.

TIP

Make sure you bring any prescription medicines that you may require, especially if you are going away for the weekend.

Life rafts

Any boat that operates more than a few miles offshore should be equipped with a Safety of Life at Sea (SOLAS)-approved life raft with the following features: canister stowage for greater long-term protection, automatic inflation, insulated floor, canopy, boarding ladder and lifelines, painter, locator lights, survival and first-aid kits, rainwater collector, drogue or sea anchor, an Emergency Position-Indicating Radio Beacon (ERIRB), and other signaling devices. The raft should accommodate the largest number of people likely to be aboard while the boat is offshore.

When purchasing a life raft, remember that an eight-person raft has room for eight people *sitting* down, not lying down. Life rafts are very hard to get into from the water and the old adage—step up into the life raft—should be taken seriously. According to life raft manufacturers, the first thing that will happen when you get into a raft is that you will get seasick, so prepare for it.

Life rafts are cumbersome, expensive to purchase, and require expensive annual inspections. But if you go out of sight of land you should have one. It could mean the difference between a mishap and a disaster.

▲ Make sure a life raft is part of your "survival kit."

PART III

MAINTENANCE

B oats, like any machines, need to be maintained or the bits and pieces eventually break. Some maintenance should be done on a weekly or even daily basis; other work can be done once or twice a year. Good maintenance can help keep the resale value of your boat high. Poor maintenance will drop its resale value by more than the cost of the maintenance. What you do is up to you, but you will enjoy your boat more if it is in tip-top shape.

CHAPTER 11

CARING FOR YOUR BOAT

To keep your boat functioning smoothly while you own it, and to maximize its resale value, it is best to follow a list of procedures during each trip and maintain all of the systems required to run the boat. Use the guidelines in this chapter to custom-design a checklist for your particular boat. Keep a record in the boat's log of all inspections, tests, and servicing of fire extinguishers.

MAINTENANCE CHECKLIST

By following the guidelines below, you can custom-design a checklist for your boat. By keeping a written maintenance log, you will create a record of all inspections, tests, and servicing that you have done.

Before You Go:

► Check the battery to make sure it is fully charged.

► Ventilate the bilge area in case there is any propane below.

► Inspect all safety gear. Make sure it is ready for instant use.

► Check that the strobe light is functioning properly (turn it upright for a minute or two).

► Turn on the electronic equipment to make sure it works.

► Stow all gear safely.

After You Return:

► Hose down the boat, trailer, and rigging after use in salt water.

► Roll or fold sails neatly.

► Clean the interior of the boat.

► Turn the battery off. Make sure the bilge pump stays on.

► Wash life jackets, harnesses, and foul-weather gear in fresh water if they've been exposed to salt water.

► Clean the boat's head by pouring the leftover dish soap down it, and then pump out the sump tank.

Once a Month:

► Inspect lifesaving equipment. Immediately replace any pieces that are inadequate.

► Check portable and installed fire-extinguishing systems.

► Scrub the hull.

► Polish and protect all stainless steel fittings and rails.

► Treat all vinyl and canvas with a preservative to prevent cracking and mildew.

- Spray exposed electrical connections with electrical contact cleaner.
- Lubricate hinges and canvas snaps.
- Check belts and hoses.
- Check battery fluid levels.
- Check all lighting for bad bulbs, connections, etc.
- Check through-hull fittings for a proper seal.
- Check drain hoses and clamps.
- Lubricate toilet seals by pouring through soapy water with a large dollop of lanolin in it.

Every Year:

- Clean and grease winches.
- Haul the boat out of the water for bottom cleaning and repainting.
- Inspect hull and fittings below the waterline—shaft, propeller, rudder, strut, and stuffing box.
- Check rigging for wear or corrosion.
- Inspect spreader attachment to the mast and to the upper shrouds for damage and cracks.
- Change fuel/water separator, if needed.
- Replace water pump impeller.
- Replace zincs.
- Check the entire fuel system inch by inch, including fuel lines in areas not normally visible.
- Have a qualified professional inspect the electrical system.
- Disconnect storage batteries and remove corrosion. Keep the batteries charged when they are off the boat.
- Discharge a fire extinguisher. Discharge and replace one of the portable units each year on a regular basis in the form of a drill with all crew members participating.
- Store electronic gear in a dry place for the winter.

The bottom isn't as easy to get to and clean as the rest of your boat. But it is most important to keep it clean because barnacles and algae can ruin the surface of your hull within weeks. In freshwater, algae and zebra mussels pose the most problems and will be the most stubborn life forms to attach to your boat. In salt water, the enemy is slime, which allows weeds to grow, which in turn provide a habitat for barnacles.

You should use a good-quality bottom paint if you keep your boat in the water. Bottom paints come in several guises. Slime-fighter paints with a biocide, such as Interlux's Ultra Kote, stop the slime from growing on your boat. If you can stop slime from growing, the barnacles do not have a layer of slime for their eggs to grip onto. If you moor your boat in waters that are heavily brackish—that is, a mixture of salt and fresh water—you should use a paint with a high copper content (some paints such as Ultra Kote have 76% copper biocide).

If you buy a new boat, your first step should be to apply a bottom-protecting paint so that you will never have an osmosis problem. Interlux's Interprotect can be applied after scrubbing the fiberglass surface of a new boat with soap and water. Then just follow the instructions on the can. In a survey done by International Paint, it was found that a boat with a bottom protected by Interprotect sold for an average of $877 per gallon of paint more than one with an unprotected bottom. In other words, if your 18-foot runabout uses two gallons of paint (costing about $60 to $70 per gallon), the resale value of your boat could be about $1600 more than that of an unprotected boat.

After applying Interprotect, you apply the bottom paint. Pick the bottom paint that is most suitable for your boat and style of boating. If you have a trawler-style yacht you can use a conventional "soft"—that is, a less expensive rosin-based—bottom paint. If you use your boat a lot, you can use an ablative paint (one in which the outer paint erodes away, exposing new bioside as it erodes). If your boat has a good turn of speed you should use a "hard" bottom paint, such as Super Fiberglass BottomKote. This paint has a 57% copper content and is especially formulated for powerboats. It can be applied up to 60 days before launching without losing effectiveness.

If you use your boat on weekends and trailer it to and from your boating area, you do not really need a bottom paint. But should you decide to use one, get a multi-use paint that allows you to launch and retrieve your boat without the paint becoming less functional when it is out of the water.

Aluminum boats should not be coated with copper-based paints. If they are, they'll turn your boat into a large battery, and could cause major damage. Aluminum boats should be coated with special aluminum paint such as Tri-Lux II. Or you can try the new Veridian paint, a silicone bottom paint with no antifouling properties at all. It is so slippery that barnacles simply slide off when the boat runs at speed. If you decide to use this paint, you'll be protecting the environment. But you need to run your boat frequently (at least once a week) to make sure the "clingons" slide off. You can also use Tri-Lux II or Veridian on your lower unit to keep it clean and unfouled. Note that Tri-Lux II does not contain Tributyltin, which has been almost completely banned because of the environmental damage it causes.

⚓ TIP
Bleach will take care of that dirty green line on your hull.

One of the reasons fiberglass boats are so popular is that they're so easy to repair. If there is a scratch in the hull, you can fix it yourself. To repair minor scrapes and scratches, use a two-part gel coat (if your boat is white). Mix the gel coat and use a plastic spatula to fill the scratch. If the damage is a little more severe, take some two-part epoxy resin such as MAS, WEST, System 3, or Epiglass, and mix it with a filler such as light-weight fairing compound, and spread it over small holes up to about half an inch in diameter.

Do not attempt large repairs unless you have had some experience using fiberglass and epoxy. Fiberglass and resins can make a horrendous mess. If you make a mistake, the only thing to do is wipe off what you can, walk away, and come back with a grinder when everything has set and grind the mess away. Grinding fiberglass is probably the most miserable job you ever want to try. Wear a Tyvek suit, a respirator, goggles, and gloves to grind fiberglass or you will itch for days. Having said that, here's how you do it:

Large holes or dents that go through the hull laminate will need to be ground back and some form of backing put in place to stop the fiberglass from collapsing. Fiberglass cloth is just like the fabric in your shirt, only a little thicker. If you try to stand a shirt on edge it will collapse, just as fiber-glass cloth will. With a support (such as a layer of masonite covered with polyethylene plastic or mold release wax) in place, a layer of fiberglass is cut to fit the hole and wetted out using previously mixed epoxy resin with no fillers. Wet out the fiberglass by pouring a little resin onto the fiberglass cloth and rolling it with a metal roller. Don't roll too hard or you will introduce airbubbles into the laminate. Keep applying fiberglass layers and wetting them out until you have built up a suitable thickness. Then let the whole mess set up. Allow at least 24 hours for the epoxy to dry and become sand-able, then sand it smooth. You may have to fill any slight holes or recesses with fairing compound until you get the entire thing perfectly smooth. Ideally you should finish up with 320 grit sandpaper to get a nice smooth finish on the entire damaged area.

If you have a spray gun you can spray on gel coat or an undercoat and then a topcoat to get an appropriate finish. The job is not easy, and getting a perfect color match often taxes a professional. In fact, pros will often paint the entire side of the hull to get a color match rather than just do a single area. If you do not have a spray gun, you can either ask a professional at your local yard to do it or try using a new brushable topside paint called Toplac. This paint is designed to be brushed onto the topsides, but it is fairly runny and you will have to be careful not to get runs in the paintwork. If you make a mistake, simply sand it back and have the yard do it.

Aluminum boats are subject to corrosion due to stray electric currents in the water. You can decrease the chance of corrosion by attaching blocks of zinc to the shaft strut. Aluminum hulls can be patched with epoxy/fiberglass patches, too. They don't usually last as long as patches on fiberglass boats, though, since metal expands and contracts at different rates than glass does.

▲ **A spray gun will help make quicker work of repainting your hull.**

Your engine, like any machine, needs care to keep it running smoothly. There are maintenance steps that you can take to make sure it's in tip-top condition at all times.

▶ Keep the belts snugly tightened. Loose engine belts begin to slip and eventually break. On outboards, this will shut down the alternators. On inboards and inboard/outboards, it will shut down the alternator, the water pumps, and the power steering. You can tighten the belts yourself by adjusting a moveable pulley, but don't overtighten it. Belts should have about 3/8 to 1/2 of an inch of flex, depending on the length of the belt. When you check the belts, look out for frayed areas. Check, too, at the bottom of the belt for signs of belt dust. This shows that the belt is misaligned. If you have any questions, get a good engine mechanic to look at it, or buy a new belt.

▶ Test the steering system for looseness or stickiness. Listen for unusual noises as you turn it.

▶ Check your steering system fairly regularly. If you feel any grinding or binding, get it checked out before you go out in the boat again. When you are helming the boat, try to judge if there is any slackness in the system. If there is, you should tighten the steering cables. Slack cables can drop off the sheaves and cause the whole thing to bind up. At the end of the season, remove the compass and store it in your basement. Lubricate the chain and sprocket gear in the pedestal. Check, too, for wear on the sprocket and chain. Once a year, check all the sheaves in the steering system. Check the quadrant and its keyway to make sure they are still tight. Fit the emergency tiller to make sure you know how to do it. After the boat is hauled, take a look at the rudder. If it drips for a long time, you may have water inside the rudder blade. If this freezes it could blow the rudder blade apart, so get it fixed.

▶ Once a year (usually when you haul out the boat) check the oil in the lower unit of all outboards. It should be dark and clear. If it is murky, it means that there is water in the unit and you should have a mechanic take a look at it. You should also take it to a repair shop if there are bits of metal in the oil. This may indicate that something is falling apart. You can add oil to the lower unit by unscrewing the oil filler screw on the bottom side of the gear housing and pumping oil into the filler hole. Make sure you wipe off any excess oil when you are done. Do not store your outboard on its side. Water can seep into the cylinder and rust everything together. Store your outboard upright.

► Retighten all loose screws, nuts, and bolts when they begin to loosen. You will need a torque wrench for most engines.

► Check your spark plugs regularly. Replace chafed plug wires.

► If you damage your prop, you will probably have damaged something else as well, so get the boat hauled and check it out. Usually, the first sign of a problem is a vibration or repeated banging on the hull. Either one could mean that you've picked up a lobster pot warp and wrapped it around the prop. If the shaft is bent (from going aground or hitting a submerged object), you will hear the noise and feel vibrations.

Washing your boat

The key to keeping your boat looking fresh and new is to wash it regularly. Except for hard-to-remove dirt, you only need to use plain old soap and water. You can scrub with a sponge on flat surfaces, but you'll need a brush on non-skid surfaces. If you wash the boat on the water, make sure you use a biodegradable soap.

Mildew in cabins and other enclosed areas can be prevented with mildew killers like Damp-Rid, No-Damp, and Lysol. On sunny days, bring cabin pads and pillows up to the deck to air out.

In the spring, polish the gel coat with a paste wax. Work over small areas until you have worked over the entire boat. Never apply the wax to any surfaces where people will be walking. Some experts recommend that when the boat is hauled in the fall it should be waxed but not polished, to help keep the topsides looking good.

Lines

Like the rest of your boat, nylon lines should be washed off after each trip and dried in the sun. Stow them in a dry place to avoid mildew.

Before storage, the lines need to be coiled. Coiling a line so that it remains tangle-free can be a tricky procedure. If it's a laid line, you'll want to coil it clockwise over your hand, giving each coil a half-twist to the right. Braided line is less likely to kink, and you don't need to twist it. Once coiled, wrap the end of the rope counterclockwise around the coils and make a small loop above the coils. Pass the bitter (in-board) end through the loop, and your coil is ready to store.

After it is cut, the bitter end of a line tends to unravel. To prevent this, tape the line where you are about to cut it and cut through the middle of the taped section. That way neither side will unravel. Either have the store where you bought the nylon line melt the end to seal it, or do it yourself with a soldering iron. You can also buy a commercial paint-like product that seals the ends when you dip the rope in it. If you do this, roll the melted end between two pieces of wood to round it off. Do not roll it with your finger, becasue the hot nylon will stick to your skin and can give you a painful burn.

> ⚓ **TIP**
> If your lines are dirty, soak them in water and dish detergent.

Sails

All sails should be rolled up or folded neatly at the end of the day. If you want to preserve the life of your sails, don't stuff them into a sailbag. Wet sails mildew fast. If you have had your sails up in wet weather, take them home and dry them on the lawn before rolling them up again.

Mainsails are usually flaked down on the boom or rolled and tied to the boom. To flake a sail, bend it zig-zag fashion in about 18 inch bends. When the sail is flaked, tie it with two or three sail ties. To prevent UV degradation, do not leave sails flaked on the boom without a sail cover. When flaking or rolling the sail, check for tears, missing stitches, corner stress lines, and delamination. Any signs of problems will give you an idea of how much life the sail has left.

> ⚓ **TIP**
> Colored sail ties stand out and ensure that you remember to remove them before the sail is hoisted again.

Trailers

Your trailer will undergo a lot of wear and tear hauling your boat from storage to water and back again. Treat it well to get the longest use possible. Every time the trailer is backed into salt water, wash it down afterwards with a solution of soap and fresh water to prevent rust and corrosion. Then spray the springs and bolts with a rustproofing spray. Allow the trailer to dry before going on the road with it or you may find that the brakes are full of water and do not work.

⚓ **T I P**

Painted steel trailers are attractive but rust easily. If you plan to put your trailer in salt water, buy an aluminum or galvanized steel trailer.

About once a month check the tires to make sure they're sufficiently inflated. Before each long pull, grease the wheel bearings. You can lock grease fittings called Bearing Buddies into the wheel hub and add the grease when needed (see illustration below). The Buddies feed the grease into the inner and outer bearings. You'll need a grease gun to force grease into the hub at the bearing fittings.

Finally, make sure all nuts on the winch and the hitch are secure and tightened regularly. All that rattling and banging regularly causes nuts to work loose.

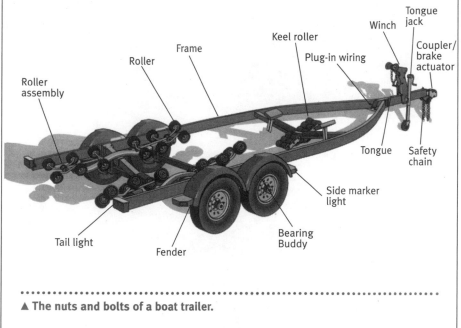

▲ **The nuts and bolts of a boat trailer.**

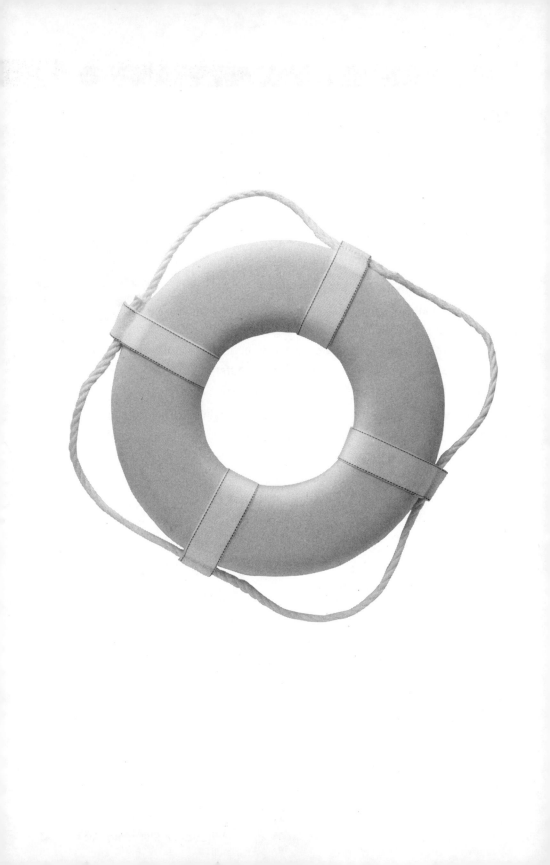

PART **IV**

TROUBLE-SHOOTING

I f you practice good seamanship procedures and maintain your boat, your sailboat experience should be relatively problem-free. **But what do you do when something really goes wrong?** Here are some of the most commonly asked questions about real emergencies—and some answers from the experts.

CHAPTER 12

EMERGENCY!

W hat do you do if there's real trouble? Despite all maintenance and the best laid plans of mice, men, and sailors, things can and do go wrong.

There are lots of reasons why your engine might not start. Let's review a few of them:

► You're out of fuel. Fuel gauges on boats are often inaccurate. Make sure that you always leave the dock with a full tank. According to tow boat service operators, their most frequent calls come from boats that are out of fuel.

► The shift lever is not in neutral. Most marine engines don't start if they're already in gear.

► The battery is dead. You can use jumper cables from your auxiliary batteries to get the engine battery going, but many boats have a switch that allows you to use your house batteries to start the engines.

► The battery wires are loose. Wiggle them to see if they're tight, and check for corrosion around the connectors. Scrape off the corrosion if you find any, and retighten the wires.

► The fuse has blown. Replace with a spare.

► You pulled the kill switch. Turn it back on.

► There's an obstruction/dirt/water in the fuel line. Check to make sure that all fittings are attached, the hose is unobstructed, the vents are open, and the filters are clean.

► It runs but doesn't shift into gear. You may have something entangled in the propeller. Tilt up the lower unit and investigate.

► Something is broken and you have a serious problem. Sail home.

If you suspect that any of these things will happen to you while you are out at sea, you would be advised to subscribe to one of the towing services. You will recoup your membership fee the first time you run out of gas.

If a fire starts on your boat, the first consideration must be for the passengers, and you should have a plan for abandoning ship if need be. If you have a gasoline explosion, there usually is little you can do except reach for a PFD and go over the side.

If you don't have to abandon ship immediately, take the following steps as quickly as possible:

► Move the boat, so that the flames blow outboard, not inboard.

► Make a radio distress call, if time permits, giving the boat's location.

► Make sure the passengers move to the safest area of the boat, such as the bow, wth their life preservers on.

► Reach for the appropriate fire extinguisher and fight the fire as described below.

▲ Pull out the extinguisher lock pin and squeeze the two handle levers together. Aim at the base of the flame with a sweeping motion; hold the stream steadily on the base of the flames until you are certain the fire is out. Dry chemical extinguishers are effective for 5 to 15 feet from the nozzle, Halon 1211 for 9 to 15 feet, Halon 1301 up to 6 feet, and CO_2 up to 3 feet.

Galley fires

According to most fire chiefs who have dealt with onboard fires, you should understand that if you cannot get the fire under control in a few minutes, you are likely to lose control of it altogether. As Chief Art Christman, of island community Jamestown, RI, says, "If you can't knock it down within a few minutes, get out of there. Your boat isn't worth your life." Boats are built of flammable materials—wood, fiberglass, and paint, and they have flammable materials onboard—fuel, oil, cooking fuel. You need to have extinguishers handy in the galley ready for immediate use.

Fires in a galley are most likely to be fueled by flammable liquids such as grease, propane, or alcohol, or by combustible solid materials such as paper, wood, or fabric. A USCG Class A, B, or C extinguisher will be effective against most kinds of fires. If no extinguisher is available, use materials at hand such as a towel to beat out the flames. If you have time to soak the towel that will be even better. Do not use water on grease or alcohol fires. If your stove uses propane for cooking, turn off the fuel supply from the tank. Once the fuel supply is cut off, let the fire burn itself out. If necessary, soak nearby wooden or fabric surfaces with water to keep the fire from spreading.

Gasoline, diesel oil, or grease fires

Use a Class B foam, CO_2, or dry chemical extinguisher. Do not use water, because it will only spread the flames.

Fires belowdeck

Fires in a vessel's cabins or lockers will most often be fueled by combustible material such as wood, paper, or fabric. You should have a Class A extinguisher mounted below, where you and your crew can get to it easily, even in the dark. If no Class A extinguisher is available, flood the fire's base with water and/or rob the fire of oxygen by closing a door or hatch to snuff it out.

Engine fires

Shut off all engines, generators, and fans sharing the engine space involved with the fire, then close any engine-room doors or hatches. If the engine-room fire extinguisher system has not discharged automatically, activate it manually. If your boat has a small specially designed aperture through which you can discharge your extinguisher without opening the engine compartment, do so as quickly as possible.

If you have one, get a crew member to prepare to launch a life raft. Get the crew into life jackets. If there is time, transmit a Mayday distress call on your portable radio. Don't stay below to use the VHF radio while a fire is raging. Use any fire extinguisher and aim it at the base of the flames.

Electrical fires

Use an approved Class C fire extinguisher designed specifically for this purpose; never use water, which conducts electricity. Fires in electrical-wiring insulation cannot sustain themselves without a great deal of oxygen; if your circuit panels are encased in a heavy metal box, in many cases closing the box will be sufficient to extinguish the fire.

What do I do if my boat springs a leak?

Turn on all electrical bilge pumps immediately, then try to identify where the water is coming in. Most leaks in fiberglass and aluminum boats will be caused by damage to through-hull fittings such as hoses, keel bolts, and underwater exhausts. Generally, your bilge pump will be able to remove the water faster than it leaks in. If you prepared your boat properly before you went to sea, you will have a suitably sized bung tied to each through-hull fitting. If any of them let go, you will be able to plug the leak with a bung and do everything possible to remove the water. If you have a really big leak (if by chance you have hit a submerged object), stuff the hole with anything available—from cushions and pillows to bedding. As quickly as possible, reinforce soft plug materials with something flat and solid, such as a hatch cover, battens, or bed slats. Once the water is coming into the boat at a slower rate than you're able to pump it out, you can head the boat to a marina or boat ramp where you can make more permanent repairs. But if you start sinking, call for assistance. Even if you don't start sinking, call and alert the Coast Guard to your problem. They need time to get help to you.

Falling overboard is a common mishap on boats. Whether it turns into an emergency depends on how quickly action is taken. Every crew should conduct man-overboard (MOB) drills on a regular basis. The priority should be getting the boat near the victim as soon as possible so that the swimmer stays in sight of those on deck.

Here are the steps you should take:

► Shout "Man overboard" and keep your eyes on the victim. Whoever sees the person go overboard should point at the person in the water and not lose sight of him or her. This crewperson should do nothing but point during the entire rescue.

► Turn off the power immediately.

► Throw the victim a cockpit cushion or life ring.

► Turn the boat toward the victim in a simple circle.

► Come in close to the victim, but not closer than ten feet. Toss him or her a life line or Lifesling. If the victim is able to swim, get a swim ladder over the side and help him or her aboard. If the victim is exhausted, injured, or unconscious, you will need two or three strong adults to lift him or her on board. If someone absolutely must go into the water to help, it is essential that he or she wear a PFD.

▲ Conduct MOB drills regularly.

WHAT TO DO IF YOU FALL OVERBOARD

Just as important as acquiring the skills necessary for rescuing a crew member overboard is knowing how to help yourself if you are the person overboard. The following tips can help you stay afloat until you are recovered.

- ► Keep your clothes on. If your shoes are light enough for you to swim in comfortably, leave them on. If they weigh you down, however, remove them. Remove any heavy objects from any pockets.

- ► If you can float on your back fairly easily, save energy by doing so. Kick only when necessary.

- ► While signaling for help or waiting for rescue, tread water to stay in an upright position, moving your hands back and forth and using a kick that requires little energy. Remember, the more you move around in cold water, the quicker your body temperature can drop and the faster hypothermia can set in.

- ► In warm water, conserve your energy by using the face-down floating technique called survival floating. Each move you make should be slow and easy.

- ► Every second counts. As soon as a heaved line reaches you, quickly tie a bowline around your chest. If a Lifesling reaches you, slip it on immediately.

- ► As the rescue boat approaches, stay away from both the stern and the bow of the boat.

- ► When trying to board the boat, don't rush; it is important to make effective use of your remaining energy.

Hypothermia is a lowering of body temperature that can occur when someone has been in the cold for a long time. The body can no longer generate sufficient heat to maintain normal body temperature. It can happen if you fall into the water, sit in the cockpit for a while on a cold windy day, or even if you are just motoring along in your boat in spring when the water and air are cool.

Mild hypothermia may include shivering and dizziness. Get the patient into a warm place and warmly dressed immediately. Moderate hypothermia includes all of the above plus a low, irregular pulse, irregular breathing, numbness, confusion, drowsiness, and apathy. The solution is to get the person warm immediately by putting him or her in a sleeping bag with hot water bottles or another person, and by getting medical attention as soon as possible.

Avoid shocking or shaking anyone with severe hypothermia. Get them to a medical professional immediately. Victims must be warmed carefully or they will die. Rapid rewarming can cause dangerous heart rhythms.

If you suspect someone has severe hypothermia, call for emergency medical services immediately. Warm the victim until medical help arrives. Get the victim out of the cold and into dry clothing. Wrap him or her in blankets and warm up his or her body slowly. Monitor vital signs and be prepared to give rescue breathing and CPR.

Heavy weather is coming

If you keep a weather eye open all the time you are at sea, you should not get caught in a storm. If you listen to NOAA weather radio, you will be able to get ashore before a storm hits unless your boat is really slow and you are a long, long way from shore. However, if you are caught by bad weather, take the following precautions:

► Secure all hatches; close all ports and windows. Put in the companionway washboards and close the hatch to keep rain and spray out.

► Remember that bilgewater adversely affects a boat's stability. Pump bilges dry, and repeat as required.

► Secure all loose gear; stow small items and lash down the larger ones.

► At the first sign of worsening weather, make sure that everyone on board is wearing a PFD.

► Break out any emergency gear that you might need—hand pumps or bailers, a drogue, etc. Use a drogue to keep the boat stern to the seas in very heavy weather or to cross a sandbar with breaking water to get into harbor. Use a sea anchor to keep the boat head-to-wind in severe conditions.

► Check your position, if possible, and update the plot on your chart.

► Alter your course toward sheltered waters if necessary.

► Reassure your crew and guests; instruct them what to do and what not to do, then assign each person a task to take his or her mind off the potential danger of the situation.

It happens to every sailor sooner or later. If you hit a soft bottom and there is no water coming into the bilge, try simply backing out first. If that doesn't work and you suspect you are on a mud bank, try blasting over the top of it. If you try to run around 180 degrees there's a good chance you'll stick tight and be there until high tide comes along. On small boats you can turn around with a pole or oar. If the water is shallow enough (most often it is only a few feet deep), simple solutions, like getting every-body out of the boat, will let the boat float free. Then you can try to push the boat off.

If getting off the boat doesn't work, try getting everyone on one side of the boat to heel it over. Often it is only the keel that is stuck, and heeling the boat works. Another technique is to take an anchor out in the direction that you went aground and set it firmly as far away from the boat as the anchor line will let you. You may be able to lead the line to your primary winches and crank the boat backwards off the sandbar. If nothing else, setting an anchor out will keep you from being driven fur-ther aground. You can also tie the halyard to the anchor line to heel the boat over and help free you. If you go aground in a river, it is often possible to take an anchor line to a nearby tree and haul yourself off, using the bow windlass or cap-stan with the outboard fully raised.

TIP
To keep from grounding, study your charts!

If you hit a rocky bottom at speed, the first thing you should do is check for hull damage around the hull/keel joint. If you have water coming into the boat, you should start the bilge pumps going. But don't worry. The boat will be high and dry and is unlikely to sink any further. Only then you can con-sider how to get your boat salvaged or towed off the rocks.

I need to be towed

If the tide is falling or a storm is rising and you can't get your boat free, it may be time to consider getting towed. You can call for a commercial towing service on your VHF channel 16. Or you can contact a passing boat. Make sure you understand the salvage forms and the relevant laws. There have been cases where boat owners who were not members of a towing organization were charged hundreds of dollars with the potential loss of their boat because they allowed the towing vessel to treat it as a salvaged boat. When a towing vessel arrives, offer your towing line and secure the tow line to the bow eye of your boat. Don't forget to tilt your drive out of the water if you have an outboard motor. If you have an inboard motor and can't tilt it, you may want to wait for a higher tide.

⚓ T I P
If you need a towing service, contact TowBoat/U.S., 800-888-4869. Or call Sea Tow, 631-765-3660.

If you are contacted to help tow someone off the rocks, make sure you know what your liabilities are. There have been cases where the operator of the rescued craft tried to make a case out of damage caused by being towed off the rocks by someone else.

My boat is swamped/capsized

A boat is "swamped" when it fills with water from over the side. Most small fiberglass boats have buoyancy built into them in the form of plastic foam flotation material. Use anything at hand to bail out the water; otherwise, hand-paddle to the nearest shore. A boat is "capsized" when it is knocked down so that it lies on its side in the water or turns over. If the spreaders are in the water, you have capsized and should be taking steps to right your boat, and shorten sail to ensure that it doesn't happen again.

Having capsized or swamped, it is important to remain calm and conserve energy. The general rule is to ensure that all crew members are wearing PFDs and that they stay with the boat. There may be possibilities of righting the boat, and rescuers will be able to find you more easily if you stay with it.

HOW DO I TRANSMIT A PAN-PAN CALL?

Send a Pan-Pan (pronounced pahn-pahn) call on VHF channel
16 or 2182 kHz (SSB) when you have a "very urgent" but not
life-threatening emergency:

1. PAN-PAN . . . PAN-PAN . . . PAN-PAN

2. ALL STATIONS.

3. THIS IS (boat name). . .(boat name). . .(boat name). . . .

4. WE (nature of your emergency).

5. WE REQUIRE (type of assistance required and other useful information such as your position, a description of your vessel, and/or the number of people on board.)

6. (Boat name).

7. OVER.

HOW DO I CANCEL A PAN-PAN CALL?

If you decide you no longer require assistance, you must
cancel the message:

1. PAN-PAN, PAN-PAN.

2. HELLO ALL STATIONS, HELLO ALL STATIONS.

3. THIS IS (boat name).

4. TIME IS (time of transmission by 24-hour clock).

5. CANCEL PAN-PAN. OUT.

HOW DO I TRANSMIT A MAYDAY CALL?

Mayday calls are the most serious radio distress call you can make and should be transmitted only in a life-threatening emergency. A mayday call means that your ship is sinking in a storm, a crew member has had a heart attack, or there is a serious fire onboard. Running out of gas doesn't qualify. Issue the call on VHF Channel 16 or 2182 kHz (SSB). You will probably have to calm yourself down to speak clearly. Try not to yell or garble your words:

1. MAYDAY. . .MAYDAY. . .MAYDAY.
2. THIS IS (boat name). . .(boat name). . .(boat name). . .
3. MAYDAY (boat name) POSITION IS (vessel position in degrees and minutes of latitude NORTH or SOUTH and longitude EAST or WEST, or as a distance and magnetic or true bearing from a well-known navigation landmark).
4. WE (nature of your emergency).
5. WE REQUIRE (type of assistance required).
6. ON BOARD ARE (number of adults and children on board AND safety equipment on board. State conditions of any injured passengers.)
7. (Boat name) IS A (boat length in feet)-FOOT (type) WITH A (hull color) HULL and (trim color) TRIM.
8. I WILL BE LISTENING ON CHANNEL (16 or 2182), THIS IS (boat name). OVER.

The act of abandoning ship is filled with potential hazards and should be undertaken only if your vessel is completely on fire or is in imminent danger of sinking. In many cases, even vessels that have been seriously damaged will remain afloat for hours or even days. Abandon ship only as a last resort. Try not to get into the water and swim to the life raft. It is very difficult to get into a raft from the water.

- ► As soon as you think you might have to abandon ship, make certain that all crew members are warmly dressed and wearing personal flotation devices.

- ► Instruct a trained crew member to stand by the life raft and prepare to launch it.

- ► Before you abandon ship, transmit a Mayday distress call and message. If no one responds, do it again. If there is still no response, try other channels. If that doesn't work, jump up and down and scream!

- ► Gather emergency supplies. If you're boating offshore, an abandon-ship bag includes signaling equipment; medical supplies; provisions, including a half-gallon of fresh water per person; clothing and fishing supplies; and an EPIRB.

- ► Make certain that your life raft is tethered to the boat, and launch it. Have one crew member board.

- ► Load the rest of your crew into the life raft, and have them fend it off from your vessel while you load your emergency gear.

- ► Activate your EPIRB as soon as you enter the raft, and leave it activated. DO NOT turn it off for any reason. Searchers will use it to home in on you.

- ► If your boat is on fire or about to sink, cut the lines tethering the raft to it. But if it is merely awash, keep the raft tethered to the boat as long as possible, playing out the full length of the raft's tether.

According to experts, the first thing that will happen when you get into the life raft is that you will become seasick. Even if you have a strong stomach, take a seasickness pill before getting into a life raft.

Glossary of Selected Terms

A

Aft: Near or at the stern.
Ahead: Forward.
Anchor rode: A line, chain, or steel cable used to hold a vessel fast to the anchor.
Astern: The direction toward the stern of a vessel, or beyond the stern.
Auxiliary: A sailboat that has an engine.

B

Battens: Thin, flexible strips of wood or plastic used in batten pockets of a sail to support (stiffen to keep flat) the roach; battens are also used in awnings.
Berth: (1) A place to sleep while on board; (2) a margin of safety, as in a "wide berth."
Bilge: The lowest point of a vessel's interior hull; also the part of the exterior between the bottom and topsides, the "turn of the bilge."
Bitter end: Inboard end of an anchor rode, the extreme end of any line.
Block: Complete assembly of sheaves or pulleys and shells (plates) on which ropes run; can be wooden, plastic, or metal.
Boom: A spar used to extend the foot of a sail.
Bosun's chair: A seat—sometimes a rigid plank, sometimes made of canvas—used to hoist a person aloft to repair rigging; pockets for tools are often included.
Bow: The forward part of a boat.
Bowsprit: A fixed spar, projecting from the bow, to which forestays and/or the headstay are fastened; also useful for anchor handling.
Bridge deck: The raised portion on top of the companionway designed to keep water out of the cabin.
Brightwork: Polished brass, bronze, or stainless steel aboard a vessel; also varnished wood trim.
Bulkhead: A traverse wall in the hull; the interior compartmentalization of a vessel is created by bulkheads; in some cases, bulkheads are watertight, in case there is damage to the hull.
Buoy: A floating aid to navigation showing channels or otherwise indicating location, rocks and other obstructions, and prohibited areas on the water; turning points in races. To buoy an anchor is to temporarily fasten the anchor line to a float, so that the anchor need not be raised when a vessel is leaving its anchorage.

C

Catamaran: A twin-hulled vessel, sail or power.
Catboat: A simple rig for a sailboat, with one mast set far forward and one sail.
Centerboard: A board or metal plate, moving vertically or pivoting up and down in a slot in the keel, which adds lateral resistance to the hull form of a sailboat; in effect the boat's sideways motion through the water is thus controlled by increasing the area of the keel.
Chain plate: Fittings on the sides of the hull or the outer edges of the deck of a sailboat, to which the port and starboard rigging, called shrouds, are fastened.
Clew: The lower, after corner of a sail, to which the sheet is attached.
Coaming: The raised edge around part or all of a cockpit that prevents the seawater from entering the boat.
Companionway: A hatch or entrance from deck to cabin.
Compass: A navigation instrument, either magnetic needles or bars attached, which floats or pivots in a bowl; older compasses used a system of graduated points, while most modern ones use the 0-360 degree system; also, a plotting tool use to draw circles or circular arcs.
Composite construction: Made with more than one component and of a different nature (e.g., plywood and fiberglass).
Cotter pin: A small pin used to secure a clevis pin and to keep turnbuckles from unwinding; a small pin used to keep any nut from backing off.
Crazing: A fine network of cracks in the surface glaze of a boat.
Cringle: A rope loop or circular eye, made on a metal or plastic thimble, used for fastening on the corner of a sail, awning, or other canvas item.
Cunningham: A line controlling tension along a sail's luff; invented by Briggs Cunningham.

Current: Horizontal movement of water, as from the normal flow of a river or when caused by the rise and fall of tides.

Custom boats: Vessels built to the buyer's specifications.

Cutter: A single-masted sailboat with mast midship, leaving room for a larger foretriangle filled by two headsails; similar to a sloop.

D

Daysailer: A boat without a cabin that is used for short sails or racing.

Dead reckoning: The navigation means used to determine position, calculated from the course steered and the speed through the water, without obtaining a fix. A dead reckoning position is indicated on a chart by marking a half circle with a dot on the track line; the time is placed at an angle to the horizontal and to the track line.

Depth sounder: An electronic depth-finding instrument measuring the time a sound wave takes to go from a vessel to the bottom and return, then displaying the result in feet, fathoms, or meters.

Dinghy: A small boat used as a tender; the term is also used for a small racing sailboat.

E–F

Electrolysis: Stray current erosion that causes weakening of through-hull fittings; may result in safety hazards or sinking.

Epoxy: Modern hull coating that enables steel and aluminum vessels to prevent electrolysis or erosion.

Feathering-type propeller: Propeller with flat blades that fold fore and aft for least resistance.

Flake down: To fold the mainsail down and tie it to the boom.

Flying jib: A third sail.

Folding-type propeller: Fixed bladed propeller where blades fold flat to reduce hydrodynamic resistance.

Foot: The bottom edge of a sail; also, to steer slightly lower than close-hauled in order to increase boat speed.

Fore: Located toward the front of a vessel.

Foredeck: The forward part of the main deck or vessel.

G

Galley: The kitchen on a boat or ship.

Gel coat: Standard finish for a fiberglass boat.

Genoa: A large overlapping jib.

Gimbals: Pivoted rings holding a compass or other device so that it can tip in any direction or remain level when the support tips.

Grab rail: A convenient grip on a cabin top or along a companion ladder.

Ground tackle: Anchor, anchor rode (line or chain), and all the shackles and other gear used for attachment.

Guys: A rigging line for control, attached to the end of a movable gear.

H

Halyard: A line used to hoist a spar or sail aloft.

Hank: A strong snap hook securing the jib to the headstay.

Hatch: A deck opening providing access to the space below; normally a hatch cover, hinged or sliding, is fitted.

Hauling out: Removing a boat from the water; pulling on an anchor line, halyard, or a rope or line is simply called hauling.

Haul out: Removal of a vessel from a boatyard for maintenance or storage.

Head: The bow or forward part of a vessel; the upper end of the vertical part, such as a rudder head; the upper corner of a triangular sail; the upper edge of a four-sided sail; the toilet aboard ship.

Headsail: Any of several sails set forward of the mast, or in the foretriangle.

Headstay: A stay from the bow to a point high on the mast; the foremost stay.

Heel, heeling: To tip, to lean to one side. Heeling may result from uneven distribution of weight or the force of the wind; a list is a continuous condition; a roll is a repeated inclination, from side to side.

Helm: The tiller, wheel, and other steering gear; a boat is said to have a weather helm if it tends to turn its bow to windward, lee helm if it tends to fall away to leeward.

Hoist: To raise up.

Horseshoe rings or buoys: A life buoy or Personal Floatation Device used in rescues; shaped like an inverted U and mounted in a bracket at the rail; used for crew-overboard situations.

Hot-bunking: Sharing a spartan bunk with someone else.

Hull: The structural body of a vessel, not including superstructure, masts, or rigging.

I–J

Idler pulley: Device used to tighten the slack in a fan belt.

J (or "The J"): The percentage of a sail's length from its headstay to the forward edge of the mast.

Jammed: Refers to a line that has been taken into a winch, wound, then locked off.

Jib: Triangular sail set on the headstay.

Jibe, Jibing: To change direction when sailing with the wind aft, so that the wind comes on a different quarter and the boom swings over to the opposite side; an accidental jibe can be dangerous.

Jiffy reefing: A reef that is tied in.

K–L

Keel: The main structural member of a vessel, the backbone; the lateral area beneath the hull that provide steering stability and reduces leeway.

Ketch: A two-masted sailing rig; the after (mizzen) mast is shorter than the forward (main) mast and stepped forward of the rudder post, so the mizzen sail on a ketch is relatively larger than it might be on a yawl.

Kevlar: High-tech sail material used in some custom-made boats.

Laminate: Thin, protective covering on the vessel's hull.

Lee: The direction toward which the wind blows; an object sheltered from the wind is "in the lee." A lee shore is the coast lying in the direction toward which the wind is blowing.

Leech: The trailing edge of a sail.

Lifeline: Usually of wire rope, often covered with plastic, at the sides of a boat's deck to keep persons from falling overboard.

Lifting keel: Sometimes called a fin keel; shaped like the fin of a fish, shorter and deeper than a full-length keel; provides greater maneuverability and "lift."

List: A continuous leaning to one side, often caused by an imbalance in stowage or a leak into one compartment.

Load: As in "under load," meaning fully loaded and equipped.

Lockoffs: Allow a line to be taken into a winch to be wound, then locked off or jammed.

Lubber's line: The index mark, usually inside the compass, by which the course is read and the vessel is steered.

Luff: The forward part or leading edge of a sail.

M–N

Mainsail (or Main): The sail hoisted on the after side of the mainmast.

Marine chandlery: A shop where nautical gear is sold.

Mast: A vertical spar, the main support of the sailing rig of sailboats; used for radio antennas and signal flags on both sail and powerboats.

Mizzenmast: On a ketch or yawl, the aftermost mast.

Mizzen sail: A small, light triangular sail attached to the mizzen mast.

Mooring: Permanent ground tackle; a place where vessels are kept at anchor.

Multihull: Any of several boat designs with more than one hull, like a catamaran or trimaran.

National Oceanic and Atmospheric Administration (NOAA): Provides the latest marine weather forecasts on weather radio channels.

O–P

Osmosis: The seepage of seawater through the gel coat of a vessel; eventually causes osmotic blistering.

Outboard: (1) A propulsion system for boats, attached at the transom; includes motor, driveshaft and propeller; fuel tank and battery may be integral or could be installed separately in the boat; (2) outside or away from a vessel's hull; opposite of inboard.

Outhaul: A line tackle or geared mechanism used to tighten or adjust the foot of a sail on a boom.

Oxidization: Occurs when the scratched outer layer of an aluminum boat reacts with oxygen to form a protective layer.

Pedestal: Base upon which is mounted the wheel or helm.

Personal flotation device (PFD): Any of several articles, such as buoyant cushions and vests or coats, "horseshoes" or life preserver rings.

Port: Left, when facing forward, as the port side of a boat, or a direction, as "to turn to port."

Preventer: A safety device that keeps a boom from swinging across the boat in a violent jibe.

Production boats: Inexpensive boats made on production lines like cars and trucks; usually of fiberglass material.

Project boat: A fixer-upper.

Prop torque: Force generated by the rotation of the propeller.

Provisioning: Loading and stocking the vessel with appropriate gear and other supplies; items needed for travel.

R

Racing dinghies: Small open sailboats used primarily for racing.

Reach, reaching: (1) to sail across the wind; (2) a channel between the mainland and an island.

Reefing: Shortening a sail; reducing the area exposed by rolling the sail on a boom or tying in reef points.

Resin: Synthetic medium mixed with a stabilizer to form the lighter, sturdier materials (such as fiberglass) used in modern boat construction.

Rigging: (1) The wire rope, rods, lines, hardware, and other equipment that support and control the spars and sails; standing rigging is semi-permanent once set up; running rigging is continually adjusted as the sails are hoisted, doused, trimmed or reefed; (2) To rig is to make a boat ready for sailing or to prepare a sail or piece of gear for use.

Roller (or rolling) furling: The method of furling a sail by winding it on a stay; most used for jibs but used for mainsails on some cruising boats.

Rolling the sail from its foot: Reefing lines to reduce sail area.

Rudder: The control surface, usually aft, by which a boat is steered.

Running fix: Determining the position of the vessel through continual reference to navigational aids.

Running rigging: Rigging that is continually adjusted as the sails are hoisted, doused, trimmed or reefed.

S

Safety of Life at Sea (SOLAS): International boating safety organization that sets standards for life rafts—size capacity ratings, seaworthiness, and sturdiness; these conventions are adapted for the U.S. by the U.S. Coast Guard.

Sailing downwind: Sailing in a direction to leeward; with the wind.

Schooner: A fore-and-aft rigged sailing vessel with two or more masts, with the foremast shorter than the mainmast.

Sea cock: A through-hull fitting with a valve that can shut off the flow of water between the boat's interior and exterior.

Shackle: A metal link fitting with a pin across the throat, used to connect lines to an anchor, fasten blocks to a spar in rigging, or a line to a sail.

Sheave: Grooved wheel or pulley over which rope or rigging wire runs; used to change the direction of force; often sheaves are parts of blocks.

Sheet: A line used to control a sail's lateral movement, either directly or by limiting the movement of a boom or other spar.

Single-handed: Sailing alone.

Slip: (1) A berth for a boat between two piers, floats, or pilings; (2) the percentage difference between the theoretical and the actual distance that a propeller advances when turning in water under load.

Sloop: The most popular sail arrangement, which has one mast forward of midship and two sails.

Sole boards: Floor boards of the cockpit or cabin.

Spinnaker: A three-cornered sail of light, stretchy cloth, usually nylon, used in downwind sailing.

Stanchion: A metal post used to hold lifelines along a deck.

Standing rigging: Permanent stays and shrouds, as well as some other rigging parts, used mainly to hold up the mast and take the strain off the sails; although somewhat adjustable, the standing rigging is not continually changed like the running rigging.

Starboard: Right-hand side of the vessel, when facing forward.

Staysail: An additional foresail that is set between the mast and the jib.

Stern: The afterportion of the boat.

Storm jib: A small, strong, triangular headsail used in heavy winds.

Storm trysail: A small fore-and-aft sail hoisted behind the foremast and mainmast in a storm to keep a ship's bow to the wind.

Styrene: For polystyrene, a synthetic material used in some molded hulls.

Suit of sails: A full complement of a boat's sails.

T

Tack: The foreward bottom corner of a sail, or either bottom corner of a square sail; each leg of a zigzag course sailed to windward or downwind.

Tacking: Sailing maneuver in which the direction of the boat is changed through the eye of the wind, often with rigging adjustment, so that the wind is coming from the other side of the vessel.

Tackle: A purchase, a block and tackle, a combination rig of one or more blocks with lines to obtain mechanical advantage.

Telltale: A wind-direction indicator mounted on the rigging, sail, or mast.

Tender: A small boat accompanying a yacht or other pleasure vessel, used to transport persons, gear and supplies; a dinghy. A vessel is said to be tender if it is relatively unstable.

Tiller: An arm or lever attached to the top of a rudder post for the purpose of controlling the position of the rudder and so steering the craft.

Topping lift: A running rigging line to control a spar; typically an adjustable topping lift would run over a sheave or through a block at the top of the mast down to the end of a boom or spinnaker pole.

Trampolining: The bouncing of fiberglass boat decks, which are flexible without being weak.

Trimaran: A boat with three hulls—a larger central hull for crew accommodation and two smaller outer hulls.

Turnbuckle: A threaded, adjustable rigging fitting, used for stays, lifelines and sometimes other rigging.

U–V–W–Y

U.S. Coast Guard (USCG): The federal marine law enforcement and rescue agency in the U.S.

Vang: (1) A tackle or adjuster that prevents a boom from lifting while sailing downwind; (2) a guy running from the peak of a gaff or derrick to the dock.

Weather helm: The tendency of a vessel to turn windward, requiring a slight amount of helm to keep it on course; normally this is considered a sailboat safety element.

Well-found: With adequate equipment and stores, well supplied and fitted out.

Winch: A device on deck, on a spar or otherwise mounted, which is used to haul on a line; if geared or used with a handle (lever) it provides a mechanical advantage.

Windage: Wind resistance.

Windlass: A special form of winch, a rotating drum device for hauling a line or chain.

Working jib: A self-tending headsail that can be controlled by one sheet rather than two.

Yacht broker: Agent working on behalf of the seller or buyer to sell or buy a boat, usually through a commission-based transaction.

Yawl: A rig for two-masted sailboats, in which there is a mainmast and a smaller mast, stepped aft of the rudder post.

Index

FOL

JUN 0 7 2024